FLASH-LIGHTS

OF

INDIA

PAST & PRESENT

FLASH-LIGHTS

OF

INDIA

PAST & PRESENT

CAPT . L . H . NIBLETT

GYAN

Published by

GYAN

Gyan Publishing House
5, Ansari Road
Daryaganj, New Delhi-110002
Phone: 011-47034999, 9811692060
E-mail: books@gyanbooks.com

Distribution Network
gyanbooks.com
India, USA, Canada, UK, Australia

ISBN: 978-93-6433-794-6 (PB)

First Published, 1930

2nd Impression 2024

Printed at: Gyan Press, Delhi.

Flash-lights of India Past & Present
Author: CAPT . L . H . NIBLETT

FLASH-LIGHTS

OF

INDIA

PAST & PRESENT

By

Capt. L. H. NIBLETT, J. P.

Price Rs. 2.

AN INDIAN RULER

Plate by kind permission of
The Fine Art College
[illegible]

FLASH-LIGHTS OF INDIA

PAST AND PRESENT

BY

Capt. L. H. NIBLETT.

CONTENTS.

WITH HUMBLE DEVOTION

THIS LITTLE WORK

IS DEDICATED

TO

F——

PREFACE.

My object in writing this little book is two-fold. Firstly I desire to place on record something of old-time India at a stage of the country's progress when the past is slipping by with enormous rapidity; secondly to enlighten people generally, and the Englishman specially, on certain phases of Indian life and customs which they largely fail to understand and, therefore, to appreciate.

It is obvious that many writers before me, with far abler pens, have touched on these subjects; but I feel I must pay my own humble tribute to a country which my family has served for three generations before me, which I have known from my earliest childhood and which has been very kind to me throughout.

My thanks are due to the Nawabs of Shamshabad for all the help and encouragement they have given me in writing the first part of the book, included in the main heading "In Mogul Harem, Tent and Court." I must mention, in particular, my friend, Nawab Syed Nawab who took the greatest interest in supplying me with material for this part of the book.

I must also express my thanks to the Editors of *The Pioneer* and the *Weekly Observer* for so kindly permitting me to publish the contents of this book in this form, the same having already appeared in their esteemed journals as articles from time to time.

For my sentiments, I make no apology: for any shortcomings, in other repects, however, I must take shelter behind a very crowded life, teeming with multifarious duties, official and otherwise, which have allowed me only spasmodic intervals to devote to this work.

L. H. N.

Why at Shamshabad ? Because it is there that the descendants of the one-time Prime Minister of the King, Nawab Fazl-i-Ali Khan, now live. They preserve to this day a diary kept for him by the son-in-law of this much-respected ancestor, and from this diary, which is partly in Persian and partly in high-flown Urdu, I have managed to glean a few incidents in the life of the King which come to us with the hall-mark of truth in that they represent a daily entry of facts, as time went on, by one who would naturally have had the best opportunity of knowing the details of the King's private life better than anyone else—except perhaps his foot-presser who was an especial favourite and during massagist operations was in a position to know even more of the monarch's private life! Let no one be surprised that the highest official of the State, whose functions should have been limited to official knowledge alone and whose connection with the King should have been a purely formal one, should have known the minutiæ of his private life. In India it was different, and, indeed, to-day it is different. The private life of high officials of the land is watched closely to the present day, and very few details are hidden from his subordinates, however much the official himself is unaware of the secret promulgation that goes on. Hardly an official visitor calls who does not first respectfully pay his respects to the orderly outside the door, pay his quota of *bucksheesh* and then receive a brief oral biography of the official's recent life which the orderly has observed himself and supplemented by the stringing together of news conveyed to him severally and jointly by the household establishment. I may be permitted here to mention *en passant*, a little conversation which took place in the Court of a Joint Magistrate while I was awaiting his arrival in court.

Enter an orderly peon bearing a *basta* (a bundle of official files tied in an immensely filthy cloth); an exchange of mutual greetings; then:—

Court Reader.—"What is the *Sahib's mizaj* (disposition) like this morning?"

Orderly Peon.—"Oh! fairly good."

C. R.—"But on what basis do you think so?"

O. P.—"Well, the *Khitmatgar* told me he ate fairly well at breakfast. He gave the bearer a slap very early in the morning for not cleaning his gun, but he seemed to quite cool down later."

C. R.—"You say he ate fairly well, but what did he eat?"

O. P.—"*Dalliya* and milk, fish, toast, eggs and bacon."

C. R.—"But that's no indication. How many eggs did he eat?"

O. P.—"I saw the bearer take two eggs in; but I don't know how many he brought out again. It was silly of me, but I forgot to take note of it."

C. R.—"But, my brother, that doesn't show anything. The point is, how many eggs does he have normally?"

O. P.—"Normally he has two and when he is annoyed, he often has none at all."

C. R.—"Now, tell me one thing more, did he have the eggs fried or——"

The Joint Magistrate's footsteps were suddenly heard and the orderly peon was found busily and assiduously dusting the table: the Court Reader, with puckered brow, reading an Urdu Order-sheet. Presumably, the conversation was continued after the Court rose for the day, but every detail was, and must have been, asked and mental notes made.

So, to return to the diary kept for the one-time Prime Minister of King Nasir-ud-din Haider, that diary's record of the King's private and public life rests upon a substantial basis.

II.—A Riverside Incident.

One of the most amusing stories in the diary is that which relates to the King's favourite foot-presser. The name of this masseur was Husaini *alias* Chichinda. The diary shows on what intimate terms Husaini was with the King, to the chagrin of the other more illustrious members of the Court. While Husaini indulged in his massagist operations he also indulged in scandalising various members of the Court and the King's ears were poisoned by these vindictive and virulent tales, so greatly resented by all and sundry. Now it came to the Prime Minister's ears that Husaini was even scandalising him to the King and he felt that the danger must be removed. So, one day, he had Husaini arrested and after castigating him roundly, he ordered that Husaini should be sent, in secret, to some remote corner of the Kingdom from where he would be unable to continue his nefarious tactics. So Husaini was duly sent, under a strong guard, to Cawnpore. Next morning, the Prime Minister approached the King with sombre face and said, "O, Roof of the World, Light of Lights, woe is me! Poor Husaini got cholera last night and though all that could be done for him was done, he expired this morning. His corpse lies there and may be shown to Your Majesty, but there is great fear of infection and should Your Majesty catch that dread disease, the rivers of your realm will swell with the tears of the people of your kingdom." The King was greatly distressed, but could not summon up the courage to call for the corpse, so he merely contented himself by retiring to his room, disconsolate and sad, and ordering that his beloved Husaini be given a splendid funeral.

The days passed by and the watch over Husaini's movements at Cawnpore became slacker. At last, one day, Husaini slipped away unnoticed and wandered back to the King's capital. Afraid of approaching the palace gates, should he be recognised and handed over to the Prime Minister, he remembered that it was the practice of the King to go out on boating expeditions in the morning during the course of which he took his daily bath. So Husaini meandered down the course of the slow-moving river and at last, he caught sight of the King in the Royal skiff, the silver panels of which were dazzling in the morning sun. The King was all alone. Slowly, Husaini approached the Royal personage. Suddenly, the King's eyes fell on Husaini, and he was astonished at the apparition that stood before him. "Husaini!" he cried "Husaini, can it be you who stand before me or is it a wraith? I thought you were dead long ago." Husaini rushed up to his old master and immediately, poured out all his troubles and told, in detail, of his banishment and the annoyance of the Prime Minister. The King was enraged beyond measure. Shaking with temper, he invited Husaini into the boat and paddled it quickly towards the palace, fuming and muttering as he went. A spy saw Husaini sitting in the King's boat which was swiftly moving up towards the palace. As swiftly, this spy sped to the Prime Minister and informed him of what he had seen and heard. The Prime Minister, trembling at the thought of his fate, quickly struck upon a plan of action, and before the King could arrive, he had issued his instructions to all the household staff. The King, followed by Husaini, now came up the steps leading to the palace, his eyes tinged with red rage, his whole frame shaking with emotion. Unable to contain himself, as he reached the palace gates, he turned on the sentry, who was standing there, and pointing to Husaini, said "Do you recognise this man? Is he not Husaini?" The sentry, true to the instructions given him by the Prime Minister, looked straight towards Husaini with blank and vacant stare and said "O, Roof of the World! O, Shadow of God! O, King of Kings! you can see all things above and below heaven, but I am a mere man, dust of dust, with only earthly sight to help me. I can see nothing." The King called him a fool, turned away and ran through the palace gates, into the throne room where, still in bathing costume, he took his seat, with Husaini by his side. He sent for the Prime Minister to appear before him immediately. Scarcely had his command gone forth when the Prime Minister appeared and bowed low, in humble homage, before the mighty autocrat in whose hands lay his life. The King looked at him and with a cruel curl of his lips demanded, "Do you know this man? Is it not Husaini?" The Prime Minister was unmoved: he looked vacantly in Husaini's direction and, nerving himself up to act the part he must play, and play well, to save his life, said with lamentation in his voice, "O, Eternal Light, have I not begged you not to go out on your bathing excursions alone? Have I not warned you that some day an evil spirit will cast its web around you? Here, you have been caught in the trammels of the ghost of the dead Husaini. You point in that direction and ask me to see Husaini and all I can see is thin air. Your Majesty, I beg you to flee from this vision that you are seeing. Compose yourself, do not allow these accursed spirits to lay hold of you." As the Prime Minister continued to speak in slow-measured and deliberate accents, the King's attitude changed; his face fell; then he seemed to be caught up in a tornado of fear and, afraid to turn his eyes again towards Husaini, lest the spirit should again cast its spell over him, he turned and fled into his *harem* for refuge. Immediately, the Prime Minister took hold of Husaini and had him marched off to his own palace. There, he decided to take his life, but later relenting, he offered him one more chance for his life and deported him to Cawnpore, warning him that should he return at any time, no mercy would be shown to him. With a view to keeping him contented there, the Prime Minister conferred upon him a small pension and the descendants of Husaini to-day are still in Cawnpore, still dependent to a greater or lesser extent on the magnanimity of the *Nawabs* of Shamshabad, the descendants of the Nawab Fazl-i-Ali Khan, one-time Prime Minister of His Majesty King Nasir-ud-din Haider.

III.—The Harem.

King Nasir-ud-din Haider could not resist a pretty face. He was, like most of the kings of those days, a much married man. Though he wore his heart on his sleeve, yet he was of a violently jealous nature. He did not even like the idea of any of his wives getting too fond of each other, and always tried to keep them apart. He was in the habit of crawling about his *harem*, at nights on all fours, to see if he could catch any of his many *Ranis* lying together. On two occasions, he discovered this, and the *Ranis* concerned were immediately put to death.

The diary, under review, mentions a number of these *Ranis* of whom I might pick out six of the chief of them, and refer to what the diary has to say about them.

His first love was Barkat Khanam, who had the title of *Afzal Mahal*. This girl was secured for the King by his step-mother for a considerable sum of money. She was presented to King Nasir-ud-din Haider while he was still a prince. She gave birth to Faraidoon Bakht *alias* Munna Jan, who was afterwards disowned by King Nasir-ud-din Haider as not being his own legitimate son. Fortunately, *Afzal Mahal* died young, otherwise she would probably have suffered for the suspicions raised in the King's heart, at a later period of his life, as regards the legitimacy of this son's birth.

His next wife was Hussaini Khanam to whom he gave the title of *Malka Zamaniya*. She was originally the wife of a *Pathan* of Benares, and worked as a maid-servant, but later, married a *mahaut* (elephant driver) in Lucknow. The star of her fortune was, however, in the ascendant and suddenly, the need arose for a wet-nurse for the infant Munna Jan, the son of *Afzal Mahal*, so this wife of a *mahaut* was given the post. She was of exquisite beauty, and no sooner did the King see her, he fell passionately in love and married her, conferring on her the title of *Malka Zamaniya* and presenting her with a *Jagir* and cash to the extent of ten lacs of rupees. Her brothers were appointed managers of her *Jagir*, and she was suddenly uplifted to Royal State, being given a retinue of a hundred elephants with gold and silver *howdas* and scores of maid-servants who, in turn, were given bullock-carts with silver trappings and palanquins of Eastern richness. How short-lived was this sudden rise to eminence however ! Only a few weeks afterwards, one Hakim Mehdi, one of the many advisers of the King, whispered to him that it was folly to bestow so much upon a woman of low birth. The King's 'love' vanished and the once all-powerful *Malka Zamaniya* was laid aside. Like a meteor in the Eastern sky, she had sped rapidly on with ever-increasing brilliancy and then suddenly that ball of fire was extinguished and lost to sight.

Then followed the Anglo-Indian wife, who was given the name of *Vilaiti Mahal*. The diary says that there was one Mr. Walters, an English tradesman, who had two daughters. Their complexion, of course, was lighter than that of the pure Indian. The diary states that one of these girls one day sent her photograph to the King and he was so captivated by it that he sent for her and married her, giving her fifty thousand rupees in cash along with ornaments worth lacs of rupees; but jealous eyes were cast on her, and suddenly, one day, an extremely cunning person, an ordinary minstrel by profession, came forward and claimed that *he* was the father of this girl and not Mr. Walters! With this claim he promptly took possession of *Vilaiti Mahal's* estate in *pargana* Mianganj. Without any enquiry, the King accepted the claim and laid *Vilaiti Mahal* aside as an impostor of illegitimate birth. No one dared ask the King either to reconsider his decision.

Next followed the daughter of a singer, Husaini, with whom the King was so much in love that he married her and called her *Khurshed Mahal*. One day, whilst fondling her, he took off his crown and put it on her head and thenceforward called her *Taj Mahal*. The diary says that a very respectable European lady of that time stated that she had never seen a more beautiful girl, either in Europe or in India, than *Taj Mahal*.

Not very long after, during the course of one of the usual revelries by night, the King was struck with the beauty of one of the dancing girls who danced before him with sinuous movements. Next day, he married her and gave her the title of *Badshah Mahal*. The King had just disclaimed Munna Jan as his son and he was filled with the desire to have an heir to the throne. He had invited *Faqirs* and *Jogis* (religious mendicants) to pray to God to grant him a son. *Badshah Mahal* seized upon this opportunity and, not very long after, declared to the King that there was every prospect of her bearing him a son in the near future. But her rivals soon betrayed her and proved to the King that if any son was born, it would not be his, but somebody else's! *Badshah Mahal* was duly laid aside.

The next wife was Bismillah Begum, to whom the King gave the title of *Qudsiya Mahal*. Of all the flimsy fascinations which the King ever had, this particular one seemed stronger than the rest. *Qudsiya Mahal* came from a Turkish family and was previously married. One day, she quarrelled with her husband and went to the palace to seek employment. She was of surpassing beauty and the King was unable to resist her charms. On hearing her story, he compelled her husband to divorce her, and married her himself. Apart from her beauty, she was most generous-hearted, even perhaps to the extent of extravagance. The diary shows that one day she asked the King to show her his collection of Kashmir shawls. Instantly, her request was granted and in a few minutes there lay on the floor before her a collection of shawls of the most exquisite beauty—the best that Kashmir could produce—the estimated value of which was 70 lacs of rupees. After going through this treasury of expensive fabrics, *Qudsiya Mahal* promptly gifted the whole collection to her maid-servants! The King was too taken aback, or perhaps, too embarrassed to protest. It is said that *Qudsiya Mahal* spent 3 crores of rupees in three years. She, too, like *Badshah Mahal*, desired to present the King with his heart's desire—a son. At last, she struck upon a plan. She secretly sent for her former husband, and he was smuggled into the palace, locked up in a box. There, he was dressed in the garb of a woman and kept in hiding. The King went into raptures when he heard he was to have a child by *Qudsiya Mahal* and he hoped that it would be a son. But the child, a boy, was still-born. The King was distracted with disappointment, and attributed this misfortune to a maid-servant, named Nooran, having cast a wicked spell on *Qudsiya Mahal*. The maid-servant was promptly put to death. Someone, however, conveyed it to the King that this boy was not his own. The King was furious. He rushed into his *harem* and laying hold of *Qudsiya Mahal*, challenged her chastity. *Qudsiya Mahal* calmly replied that if he suspected her chastity, she was prepared to lay down her life at his feet as she had promised to do when she married him. The King laughed cruelly at this and retorted, "so said many others before you, but it's easier said than done." Like a flash, *Qudsiya Mahal* whipped out a dagger from her waist and plunged it deep into her heart. There, at the King's feet, she breathed her last. This was on August 21st, 1834.

Let us now draw a veil over the *harem* and its tragedies.

IV. –The Court.

We have seen how the *Ranis* in the *harem* fared—to-day at the zenith of their glory; to-morrow, laid aside and forgotten. But it was not only in the *harem* that we observe these meteoric ascents and descents in the Royal favour. In the Court, the same régime prevailed.

The diary, under review, mentions the case of one Ram Dayal. He was the son of one Beni Ram, a barber by caste and a betel-nut seller by profession, who had two wives—one a Hindu and the other a public woman by the name of Ashooran. Ram Dayal was born of the Hindu wife. Ashooran had a daughter by Beni Ram. This daughter grew to be an extremely captivating girl and Ram Dayal (her half-brother), hoping to make a good thing out of it, presented her to King Nasir-ud-din Haider. The King was so pleased with her that he married her and conferred the title of *Phul Mahal* on her. But this was not all. Ram Dayal had to be rewarded. The title of 'Raja' was conferred upon him and he was made *Madar-ul-Moham* or Chief of the Household Staff—a position from which a maximum income could be extracted with the minimum effort—that effort being merely the preparation of a bill for household expenses. Whether all the items in that bill were strictly correct was, of course, of minor importance, but the *time* of presentation of the bill was all-important. To receive immediate sanction, it was necessary to place it before the King for scrutiny at a time when his vision, as well as his understanding, was blurred by drink. At such a time, the King signed a payment order for a couple of lacs of rupees with as much exultation as he would crack a vulgar joke.

In the Court, the gamble for power always prevailed. Any vulgar comedian who had sufficiently attracted the attention of the King could meddle with State matters. It was a Court mimic, Fazl-i-Ali, by name, who, at a time when the King was guffawing uproariously at an obscene joke, suggested a successor to the Prime Minister and promptly his proposal was accepted. Hakim Mehdi Ali Khan, the nominee of the minstrel, was duly appointed Prime Minister! Nevertheless, Hakim Mehdi Ali Khan was a very able man and, besides reorganising the law and police departments, he set the State finances on stable ground. He increased the State revenues and cut down expenditure to a minimum.

The 'axe' was applied even to the King's personal requirements; cloth which was bought for the King's *paijamas* was usually valued at Rs. 50 per length, but the new Prime Minister bought it at Rs. 15 a length. Handkerchiefs usually purchased at Rs. 3 each were now bought at Re. 1 each. The King was in the habit of discarding any article of clothing he had used once. Hakim Mehdi Ali Khan ordered that these articles should be washed and worn at least three times before being discarded. On one occasion, the King ordered 500 gold bracelets to be distributed amongst the maid-servants of the *harem*. The Prime Minister secretly had the bracelets made of silver and washed over with gold. But this was his downfall. The King resented thrift and was greatly displeased with the Prime Minister's niggardliness. Finally, it took a card-sharper, Taj-ud-din Husain Khan, to recommend and obtain his dismissal.

It was during the Premiership of Hakim Mehdi Ali Khan that there was another dramatic example of a rise to power and a sudden fall from the zenith of favour. It happened thus. While the King was holding Court one day, a lunatic burst into the chamber with a loaded gun on his shoulder and a naked sword in his hand. He sprang at the King and a servant, Mamman Khan, who was standing nearby, grasped the lunatic by the back of the neck and overpowered him. The King was in a cold sweat with the suddenness of this onslaught and, with a heart overflowing with gratitude and admiration, he immediately appointed Mamman Khan a courtier of the front rank of favourites. Mamman Khan, being of low estate, did not bear his elevation with the grace he should have, and, taking advantage of the Royal favour, continued with greater nonchalance to indulge in all the city brawls and *bazar-riots* in which he could possibly partake. The Prime Minister complained against him to the King; but no serious notice was taken. This increased the presumption of Mamman Khan and he then attempted to undermine the influence of the Prime Minister. One day, in open Court, he spoke in the foulest language of Hakim Mehdi Ali Khan. The King overheard it and taking it to be as contemptuous of his presence as it was insulting to the Prime Minister, he ordered the arrest of Mamman Khan. With kaleidoscopic rapidity, Mamman Khan fell. His days were numbered. But he was not to escape with a normal death. The King delegated his power to the Prime Minister to decide the form of death. The lust for revenge ran riot in Hakim Mehdi Ali Khan's breast and, like a flash, he made his pronouncement. "Let him be hanged by his legs, head downwards," said Hakim Mehdi Ali Khan in measured accents, while the Court was silenced in expectation. "And," continued Hakim Mehdi Ali Khan, "let the heaviest pair of pincers available in the Kingdom be clamped upon his wicked, lying tongue till it is drawn out of his hideous head." The King paused a moment, and the whole Court listened with bated breath, to hear whether the King would accord his Royal sanction to this form of torture and death for a one-time favourite and a saviour of the Royal personage. It was a pause of only a moment and the King, with a voice which could hardly be heard even in the death-like silence which prevailed, said hoarsely, "Let it be done" and hastened from the throne-room into his *harem*. Before the day was done, Mamman Khan had paid the terrible penalty and was dead.

V.—The King's Joke.

It was an early summer morning when King Nasir-ud-din Haider was walking in the cool of his garden. He stood for a while before the fountain and watched the morning sun bursting through the spray in varicoloured tints. Through that veil of rainbow colours he saw a shadow flit past from one evergreen shrub to another. What could it be? A man, a murderer, a spy on his *harem?* All these questioning thoughts must have flashed through his mind surcharged with dark suspicion. "Come here, Badmash (villain)" he called, "come forth at once and explain how you lurk here." The figure emerged quiveringly from behind the shrub. He was ragged and poorly-dressed, with dishevelled hair and beard. Hardly had he approached within 20 paces of the King, when he prostrated himself on the ground muttering, "O! Roof of the World, Protector of the Poor, Worshipful Presence—mercy." "What brings you here, blackguard?" demanded the King.

"My brother is in your service, Your Majesty," cried the prostrate man. "He is Razzak, groom, and I came here to look for him and ask him to help me to get employment in Your Majesty's stables. I am a stranger here and lost my way, never dreaming that I would insult Your Majesty's eyes with the vision of so miserable a sight as myself." The King realised that the man was perfectly honest, but always fond of a joke, dissembled anger and increased suspicion. "Villain!" he cried, "You lie! Murder is written in your face, and I take your presence to mean treason. You shall be put to death."

At that moment, one of his servants, with consternation in his eye, approached the King. "Bring me my pen and a scroll of paper. I shall write this man's death warrant." "Mercy! Mercy!" cried the man, in broken accents of agony and apprehension. Immediately, the pen and paper were at hand. The King proceeded to write while his victim continued to writhe and cry in the acuteness of his suffering. "Give this man a post on Rs. 5 a month," he wrote and rolling up the paper, with a grim smile, he handed it to his servant. "Give this," he said to the servant, "to the Royal guard and order them to send this man immediately, under escort, to the Prime Minister who will carry out my orders at once." The prostrate man, still pleading for mercy, was immediately conveyed from the scene, and hardly had he gone, when the King was convulsed with laughter.

The Prime Minister at that time was Nawab Mir Fazl-i-Ali Khan (whose son-in-law's diary we are perusing). He was unable to reconcile the pitiful cries of the supposedly condemned man with the terms of the order he had received. So he wrote a note on the scroll explaining the circumstances to the King and asking if there was some mistake about it. The King, on receipt of the enquiry, merely passed a line through the Prime Minister's remarks and added a dot after the figure "5" in his order, which made it read in the vernacular, "Rs. 50." The Prime Minister was still more confused on receipt of this and thinking that someone was befooling him, wrote back again by a special and trusted messenger of his own, asking the King whether these were his orders. Again, the King passed a line through his remarks and added another dot to his order. "Give this man a post on Rs. 500

a month" was what the order now read! Dumb-founded, Nawab Mir Fazl-i-Ali Khan hastened to the Palace himself and explained to the King that if there was no mistake and the order was meant to be carried out to the letter, the Royal coffers were so empty that this would be increasing the strain upon it for the sake of an employee who would be worthless in any capacity. "*Nawab Sahib*", replied the King, "You are right. There *is* a mistake. Give me the *parwana* (order)." Taking the scroll, he chuckled to himself and added yet another dot after the previous figure making it read "Rs. 5,000 a month." "The mistake is now rectified" he said. The Prime Minister bowed in obeisance and was departing, when the King added, "Now, convey my order to the man and send him to me." The Prime Minister obeyed the Royal command and soon the ragged man stood before him, as in a dream, unable to understand what would be the end of these developments, unable to realise what the real object of the King was. "Release him", said the King to the guard, and the shackles which bound him were removed. Then, turning to the released prisoner, the King said, "Your thanks are due to the *Vazir* (Prime Minister) for your promotion from Rs. 500 to Rs. 5,000 a month. Go now, and when the Court opens to-day, you will be created a *Nawab*." The surprised man *salamed* deeply and was on the point of backing away from the Royal presence, when suddenly the King turned and spoke again. "But wait; you cannot go like that! It would be a disgrace to the position you now hold." He then sent a servant to have the man bathed and groomed and ordered that some of his own clothes should be put on him. In half-an-hour, the stranger was present before His Majesty, apparelled in garments of the richest brocade. "Now," said the King "You may go." And then, again, he checked the stranger. "But wait; you cannot walk in the streets like that! It would be a disgrace to the position you hold." Immediately, he ordered that a troop of Cavalry should be given him as a guard of honour, a retinue of 30 servants for personal attendance and 20 elephants, gaily caparisoned, to convey the new dignitary and his staff to the Palace vacated by the previous Prime Minister and now assigned to this new power in the land. And so, the gorgeous procession proceeded on its triumphal march. An hour later, it retraced its footsteps to the Court, where in Royal State a new *Nawab* was created and a new star scintillated—for a while—on the Mogul horizon. But it was only for a while, and the mighty power fell. Along with it fell also Nawab Mir Fazl-i-Ali Khan who was grossly insulted in open court by having his turban knocked off his head at the instigation of the King.

Shakespeare might have been peering into these scenes of fallen glory when he wrote those memorable lines :—

> " And, like the baseless fabric of this vision,
> The cloud-capp'd towers, the gorgeous palaces,
> The solemn temples, the great globe itself,
> Yea, all which it inherit, shall dissolve,
> And, like this insubstantial pageant faded,
> Leave not a rack behind. . . . ."

So it was in the time of King Nasir-ud-din Haider—in that shadow-land where men and women had such frail and delicate hold of position and power, and existence itself.

VI.—The Camp.

On one occasion, the King was proceeding to the *jungles* of his kingdom for *shikar*. A gorgeous procession was formed and the King was mounted on the leading elephant which was heavily caparisoned with gold, and carried two huge silver bells on either side which tolled with every step the leviathan animal took. Above him, there dazzled, in the bright sunlight, a richly-brocaded red umbrella. A troop of brilliantly-uniformed Cavalry, with brightly-coloured pennants flowing from their glistening lances, led the procession. Behind the King's elephant, there followed a great host of richly-draped elephants and palanquins bearing the King's staff and dancing girls.

The streets were packed, and great crowds gathered to see the Royal monarch pass on his way from the palace.

Suddenly, the King's eyes fell on a man making faces at him. He stopped his elephant and ordered the man to come forward. All eyes were set on the man as he came, and those who had seen the offence committed, thought that nothing could avert an order for the man to be put to death instantly. The man realised his own danger, and immediately commenced to dissemble lunacy. Turning to the Prime Minister, who was on the elephant next following, His Majesty, the King said "Let this man be taken to the Master of Ceremonies and placed first on the programme of entertainment for to-night. He will make facial contortions for an hour in my presence and if he is not sufficiently funny, he will be put to death." The order was obeyed and the man was taken, in chains, to the camp.

That night, this man, with the shadow of death before his face, had to indulge in varied forms of grimace to tickle the fancy of the King and thus escape the awful fate that awaited failure. He succeeded, and was thereupon, appointed permanently to entertain His Majesty.

The King had been two days in camp when the Prime Minister, Raushan-ud-daula, happened to mention that the *shikar* had cost 15 lacs of rupees and that now, the Royal coffers were empty. What seemed to have happened was that the personal exchequer of the King which he had inherited from his forefathers had been drained dry by the King's extravagance. The State balance had been spent by Raushan-ud-daula and could not, therefore, be used to replenish the former. The King was furious and, fuming with rage, he ordered that the camp should return at once and that it should reach Lucknow by noon the following day. It was then midnight, and Lucknow was 40 miles away. A palanquin was ordered for the King and within ten minutes, the procession started back; the brilliant lights of the Royal tent were extinguished; the whole scene was one of activity as tent after tent dropped with heavy thud and was folded up and packed away. Before the darkness was out, the grove which had presented so resplendent an appearance but a few hours before, was deserted. Dawn broke to see a plain littered with straw and broken pitchers, with no signs of life anywhere. Such were the whims of King Nasir-ud-din Haider.

The King brooded about this incident and his temper grew exceedingly bad. His capriciousness was more marked than ever. He began to drink even more heavily than before. One night, while the revelry of the Court was in full swing, he got annoyed with the dancing girls who were doing their utmost to please him and to vie with each other. For a time, the King had enjoyed their boisterousness and had even encouraged them to go on. With minds ablaze with drink and hearts excited with jealousy of each other should one be favoured more by the Royal pleasure, these seven girls danced on, becoming more turbulent with every step. The music was at its height. Suddenly, the King frowned ominously. The next moment, he raised his hand in signal for the revelry to stop. The music was silenced, the dancing and buffeting ceased. "Is this your respect for my Court and my presence?" he thundered. "Are you here for my pleasure or to tear yourselves to pieces like wild-cats? If it is the latter, you want, you shall have it." Saying this, he ordered the seven dancing girls to be locked up in a room measuring 10ft. × 10ft. with no ventilation, the door to be chained from outside. It was a terrible June night. The girls, hot from their violent exercise, ablaze with the fire of liquor burning within them, were forcibly incarcerated, in this tiny room with no inlet for air. At first, wild shrieks emanated from within; then low cries for water, then moaning, then silence. Next morning, the seven corpses found in the room were buried in the same grave outside the Palace gates. They were mere girls of ages ranging from 14 to 17 years; but what of that? There were many others like them in the Royal Court of King Nasir-ud-din Haider.

VII.—The King's Bravest Act.

There was no indulgence in which the King entered more heartily than that of watching elephant fights. He would sit on the balcony of his palace at Musa Bagh and look over the silent waters of the Gomti, on to the giant arena across the river which was prepared for the purpose. The people gathered in their thousands to witness these mammoth contests. One day, a terrible tragedy occurred. After a vicious fight, in which two enormous brutes engaged, the victorious elephant, maddened with rage, stinging with pain from his lacerated wounds, excited by the bedlam created by the massed throats of thousands of spectators, filled with the fire of victory, ran amok. Like the players of a victorious team throw up their hats in delight and exultation, the triumphant elephant picked up men and women from the massed sides of the arena and flung them skyhigh, trampling them to death as they fell. Others, he caught and tore limb from limb. It was some time before the crowd could recede in their frantic flight. Not satisfied with this individual damage, the elephant now commenced to tear up booths which crashed to the ground with a hundred terror-stricken spectators upon it. Then, from across the river, the King's bodyguard, seeing the awful wreckage, raised a cry of horror. The elephant heard it and, breaking through the arena, with trunk upraised, made for the water's edge. In a minute, he was swimming furiously and fast across the river, in the direction of Musa Bagh. The King noticed this, and ordered his lancers to prepare to meet it with a charge. Soon, the elephant had gained the opposite bank and with a hollow blood-curdling shriek, made for the palace. The lancers charged, riding knee to knee, in solid phalanx, their pennants fluttering in the air. The elephant veered and received only a few glancing spear-wounds from the flank of the charging troop. He then, turned back towards the river-bank and attacked those who were fleeing hither and thither to save themselves. It was then, the King showed remarkable courage. He hastened down the steps and in spite of all entreaties by his advisers, mounted his snowy-white Arab and unarmed, galloped, at tremendous speed, towards the death-dealing giant. Risaldar Mustafa Khan Kandhari alone, followed him. Then, a miracle happened. The elephant—whether it had cooled down by this, or whether even with its brute-mind, it realised that it was Majesty itself which approached him or whether it had respect for an unarmed horseman—dropped his trunk from its upraised position and looked meekly at its assailant. The King drew up within a few feet of it and then walking his horse up to the monstrous beast laid hold of it by the ear. Slowly, he brought it back to the palace gate and made it over to its *mahaut*. The people were struck dumb with amazement, and it was not till the King was seen again on his balcony, that a roar of applause went up from the thousands who were gathered around.

VIII.—The End.

Distraught at the death of his favourite queen, *Qudsiya Mahal*, haunted by the phantom of impending bankruptcy and soured by bad health, the King now became increasingly morose. He took a vow that he would live the life of an ascetic for the rest of his days. He discarded his bed with its voluptuous cushions and silks, and slept on the floor which was covered with velvet mattresses and Persian carpets. To imitate the garb of a dervish, he ordered more shawls from Kashmir, the value of which ran into several lacs of rupees.

One day, the Prime Minister of that time (Raushan-ud-daula) remarked to the King, " Sire, while Your Majesty frets so for the death of the *Rani Sahiba* (*Qudsiya Mahal*), your step-mother (*Badshah Begum*) lives a richer, brighter life each day on the hidden treasures in her palace. She mourns not at all." To add fire to this, a maid-servant, who was standing by, added "Well, a step-mother is after all only a step-mother. Had she been a real mother, she would surely have shared Your Majesty's griefs with you." The King rose from his melancholic stupor and with never a word, proceeded to *Badshah Begum's* palace. As soon as it came to be known that the King was proceeding there, some mischief-makers, with a desire to fan the fire, posted two eunuchs, armed to the teeth, at *Badshah Begum's* house. The King noticed them and took it as a sign of defiance to himself. He rushed into the palace and demanded that *Badshah Begum* should leave the house at once and also surrender Faridoon Bakht to him. The Mogul spirit rose within

Badshah Begum's breast and drawing herself up, with a flash of challenge in her eye, she refused to comply with any of the King's demands. "When I was bold enough," she said, "to disregard your father's authority, do you think I will cower before his son whom I have brought up in my arms?" Afraid of what the Governor-General would do if he interfered with his step-mother, still fuming, the King withdrew; but later he made up his mind to evict *Badshah Begum* by force.

A few days after, he called up part of his army and ordered General Raja Darshan Singh and General Sheo Dan Singh to take possession of the palace by force. They marched on the residence of *Badshah Begum* and besieged it. The *Begum's* personal bodyguard was overpowered, arrested and imprisoned; but the Begum herself, accompanied by her maid-servants, were not prepared to yield without an effort. So they, suddenly, emerged from the palace, armed with brick-bats, and showered these with vehement force on those who stood at the gate. Raja Darshan Singh was rather severely wounded and so taken aback were his men, that they retired to the gates. Then, all unexpected, they were suddenly fired upon by some of the *Begum's* bodyguard who were hidden inside the house. This led Raja Darshan Singh to return fire and as a result, four negresses and many maid-servants of the *Begum* were killed. At last, the *Begum* asked for quarter and was allowed to leave the palace in peace and take up her residence in Almas Bagh.

A few days later, the King regretted his action and went to his step-mother's to ask pardon of her and to beg her to go back to her palace. *Badshah Begum* was in tears and besides forgiving the King, asked him to stay the night there as it was too chilly for him to go back to the Palace. Unable to do enough for him, the *Begum* gave him her own feather quilt to cover that night and asked him to keep it as a gift. The King accepted the quilt.

The next morning, when the King returned to his Palace, he told his Prime Minister, Raushan-ud-daula, what had happened and how glad he was that he and his step-mother were again on good terms. But Prime Ministers in those days dreaded unity in the Royal family because they always could make more out of disunion. Raushan-ud-daula, therefore, dissembling horror, exclaimed "For Heaven's sake, Your Majesty, beware of the impending danger. Your Majesty's step-mother has appointed four negresses with the special purpose of poisoning you. But for the efforts of the eunuch I sent to protect you last night, you would have been a dead man by this."

To a weak mind like that of the King, haunted by suspicion at every turn, influenced by every soothsayer and adviser, the King believed the crafty Raushan-ud-daula and flying into a rage, consigned his step-mother's quilt to the flames.

The *Begum* was both distressed and alarmed to hear of the fate her gift had met and wondered what the King's next move would be. Lest he should attack her again with his Army, she started recruiting a force of her own. In a few days, she had collected nearly nine thousand soldiers around her. On hearing this, the Resident (of the East India Company) was alarmed, and to avoid further bloodshed, asked the *Begum* to disband her Army. The *Begum*, however, replied that she only retained them for self-protection; but the Resident insisted, and even offered that any salaries due to them for the period of their employment would be paid from the Royal Exchequer. The Resident then wrote to the King saying that he had settled the matter and that the King should pay a sum of Rs. 15,000 a month to his step-mother as a maintenance allowance and also two lacs in a lump sum to her Army, which would be disbanded immediately. The Resident's letter reached the King that evening and he issued directions to the Prime Minister to put up a payment order before him the following morning for his signature, authorising the withdrawal of the money from the State coffers.

Dawn broke: the King lay motionless in his bed: the curtains were drawn: the King was dead. And courtiers in hushed voices, whispered the word 'poison' to each other in the far corners of the death chamber.

Thus, passed King Nasir-ud-din Haider at the early age of 35, almost exactly a century ago.

CAMP SONGS.

I.—Morning.

The air of the morning towards me is wafting
Its scent with its sweetness and freshness and cheer,
The night with its sighing and sorrow and crying
Is gone with its harrowing darkness and drear
The birds they are warbling, the camels are burbling,
The dawn it has tinged with its silver the night,
The dogs they are baying, the horses are neighing,
The fiat of heaven is "Let there be light".
The well it is creaking and thus it is speaking
Of life-giving water that's drawn from its bowl,
The cattle are lowing as slowly they're going
O'er the russet-brown plain with tinkle and toll
The rustic is singing his song of the morning,
The mist it is lifting its ashen-grey pall
The tents all a-glimmer the dew-drops a-shimmer
The Sun, in its brightness envelopes them all.
Our hearts they are voicing their buoyant rejoicing
At the wak'ning of life at birth of the morn,
Our lips, they are whisp'ring, their praise they are lisping
To Him Who with splendour this earth did adorn.

I.—Evening.

The camp-fires are burning, the night is returning,
The long day of toil and of labour is o'er,
The shadows are stealing across the blue ceiling,
Of the camp and the grove, the plain and the moor.
The night-wind is sighing and singing and crying
Through the trees, its weary sad anthem to Night;
The stars they are gleaming, the Moon's softly beaming
As onwards she speeds on her nocturnal flight,
The jackals are howling, in packs they are yowling,
A lone hungry wolf breaks the night with his shriek.
These sounds of weird crying are rapidly dying,
Now silence holds sway o'er the camp and the creek.
A voice it is pleading for heavenly leading,
'Tis the voice of a fear-filled and frail human soul
As this Globe keeps spinning, now losing, now winning,
We're slowly but surely approaching Life's goal.
Dear Master of Evening and Lord of the Morning,
Through the night with its doubts, its dangers and fears
We'll lie safely sleeping secure in Thy keeping
And cast upon Thee all our cares and our tears.

INDIAN FESTIVALS.

I.—The Meaning of *Dasehra*.

WE have come to think of *Dasehra* only in terms of holidays, vacations and reduced railway fares; but what is the elemental significance of *Dasehra?* What is the meaning of this religious observance? We have only to look into the *Ramayan* to see that *Dasehra* is at once a sermon and an entrancing story of adventure and self-sacrifice and love.

A million years ago, there reigned over the Kingdom of Uttra Kosul the great *Chattri* king, Dasarath. His capital was at Ajodhia, a city which reared its head in grandeur overlooking the Sarju River near the present city of Fyzabad. The glories of this kingdom have been sung by Hindu bards and minstrels for centuries past and some of the lore has come down to us of the present day. I heard an ignorant cultivator describe the limits of that kingdom in the following lines:—

> "Púrab marey Pur Paṭan tak,
> Pachhim marey Bind pahár,
> Dakhin marey gaṛh Kábul tak,
> Uttar—sáṭh khanḍ Naipal."

His Geography was all wrong of course, but the limitations given suggest a vast kingdom.

Dasarath had three queens. His eldest son was Ram, who was born of the senior queen. His second son was Lachhman, born of the second queen, and his third and fourth sons, Bharat and Shattrugun, were born of Kaikei, the third queen.

One day, as Dasarath stood before a mirror in the Palace, he observed that his hair was turning grey and he decided that the time had come when he should go into retirement from worldly affairs. He resolved to abdicate in favour of his eldest son, Ram, who was particularly precious to him. All arrangements were made and an auspicious day was fixed for the coronation.

When the news reached Queen Kaikei, however, she was extremely envious that one of her sons should not be given the throne.

Now, Dasarath had promised Queen Kaikei long years before that he would be prepared to grant her any two requests she would make of him at any time. Queen Kaikei had remembered the promise and now felt the time had come to use the privilege to advantage. She reminded King Dasarath of his pledge and demanded that her son, Bharat, should be given the throne and that Ram should be banished to the outermost forests of the kingdom. Torn between his pledged word on the one side, and the love of Ram on the other, Dasarath was distraught. To a *Chattri* of those days, however, the breaking of one's word of honour was a most contemptible and unpardonable act. After a tremendous mental struggle, he decided to keep his promise and issued orders in accordance with Queen Kaikei's request. With breaking heart, he told Ram he must go into the forest for a period of 14 years, knowing that he could never withstand the separation. Ram obeyed meekly but resolutely, taking leave of his parents. Along with Ram went Sita, his beautiful wife, and

Lachhman, his devoted step-brother. At the time, Bharat was away on the North-West Frontier visiting his mother's ancestral home and all unaware of the arrangements his mother was making for him at Ajodhia.

Dasarath could not survive the consuming sorrow of parting with his beloved Ram and very soon after, pined away and died. The funeral ceremonies had to be performed by one of his sons. Ram and Lachhman were untraceable in the distant forests, so Bharat was sent for. He performed the funeral rites and was then asked by his mother to ascend the throne.

Now, Bharat was an extremely right-thinking young man and when he heard of the manner in which his mother had paved his way to the throne, he was greatly annoyed. Denouncing the action of his mother and deploring the banishment of Ram, he proceeded into the forests to find the exiles and bring them home. Deeper and deeper into the forest he went in his search till at last, on the hills of Chittra Kot, he caught a glimpse of three wandering figures. He bowed down in obeisance as he approached Ram and begged him to return to Ajodhia. Ram, however, was absolutely firm on the point that he would not disobey his father's orders and not until 14 years was complete would he place foot in Ajodhia. Unable to persuade him, Bharat took from Ram's foot his sandal and going back to Ajodhia, he placed this on the throne and ruled the State in Ram's behalf, awaiting his return.

Ram now proceeded further and further south till he was somewhere in the vicinity of Rameswaram. One day, he found his wife, Sita, missing. Lachhman and he started a vigorous search, but failed to find her. At last, they met the monkey-god, Hanuman, who helped them to trace Sita's whereabouts. She had been forcibly abducted by Rawan, King of Lanka (Ceylon) and imprisoned because she refused to marry him. On hearing this, Ram collected a great army of Southern India aborigines called 'Banars', and marched towards Lanka. Before he could reach his objective, he was met by Rawan and a sanguinary battle ensued, Rawan being killed in the fray. Thus, was Sita restored to Ram, and it is this battle which is commemorated at *Ram Lila* festivities when towering paper effigies of Rawan are burnt.

That is the story of *Dasehra*, but what a lesson it has, not only for the Hindu mind but for the world! Do we merely see the victory of Ram over Rawan or do we see through it and behind it, the triumph of virtue over evil, of truth over falsehood, of soulful submission over worldly desire? We see, personified, the obedience of a son, the faithfulness of a wife, the loyalty and self-sacrifice of brothers and the love of a noble father—all wrapped together in one grand conception. Is it any wonder then, that the Hindu mind is stirred by these historical facts and that the Hindu heart is softened with the beauty of the character of these heroes? It is thus that, at *Dasehra* time, when the colossal Image of Rawan bursts into flames and crashes to the ground two hundred million Hindu voices cry, "Jai Sita Ram!" Victory to Sita and Ram! Victory to Honour over Dishonour! Victory to Right over Wrong!

This is *Dasehra*.

II.—*Diwali* : The Festival of Light.

Diwali is the Festival of Light. It is celebrated on the darkest night following *Dasehra*, mid-way in time between new-moon and full-moon, and commemorates the return of Ram to ascend the throne of Ajodhia after his 14 years of exile in the forests of his kingdom. His arrival was awaited by a vast concourse of subjects who gathered round the throne waiting in anxious expectation for the advent of their King. Then, through the brushwood and the forest, emerged the mendicant King, saffron-clothed, barefooted and bareheaded, with a sheaf of arrows across his back and a giant bow in his hand. All Ajodhia went mad with transports of joy. The Capitol and the Kingdom alike, welcomed their King with jubilant acclamation. Ram ascended the throne which had lain vacant for him through that long period of time. Timbrel and cymbal, *dholak* and *sarangi*, vied with each other to fill the air with music worthy of the occasion. Thus passed the hours of "*Raj Gaddi*" day, the day of enthronement.

Night came. A thousand flares went up in old Ajodhia. A myriad lights scintillated in the darkening sky and made day of night, while the warrior King sat in Royal State, in the splendour of his simple regalia. There sat a victor over mighty Rawan; a victor over personifed Wrong; nay more, a victor over himself. Had he not met temptation and conquered it! Had there not been placed before him, with entrancing imagery, the vision of the throne of Ajodhia should he but decide to mount it, forgetful of his father's command that for 14 years he should remain a wanderer on the face of the earth with the trees of the forest for his canopy and the cold, bare ground for his bed. There sat Ram, listening to the temple-bells which rang out into the night-air, listening to a chorus of hautboys and conches that bellowed forth their message of welcome, listening to the murmuring refrain of the multitude who had gathered outside the Palace gates and massed themselves together in every street and every public resort within the city walls.

Those glimmering lights that shone out in serried lines, had a dual significance. They constituted the outward sign of jubilation and welcome; but they also operated as a means of driving away the powers of darkness which, in unseen and intangible shapes, hover around scenes of grandeur on the most auspicious occasions. That belief held sway in Ajodhia as it held sway in Ancient Rome. It is that belief which the great Plutarch recorded and which Shakespeare put into the mouth of Horatio, the Danish courtier, with ominous significance, as he stood on his night-watch just before the ghost of Hamlet's father re-appeared :

"In the most high and palmy state of Rome
A little ere the mightiest Julius fell,
The graves stood tenantless and the sheeted dead
Did squeak and gibber in the Roman streets."

It was these precursers of future ill-fortune, these

". . . . harbingers preceding still the fates
And prologue to the omen coming on"

that the people of Ajodhia wished to keep away from their beloved sovereign and King.

In the course of the centuries which have passed, other observances have come to be recognised in connection with

Diwali. To some, it is a restival which connotes cleanliness, and the occasion is observed by white-washing, dung-coating and repairing the home. All the collected rubbish is then conveyed to the village dung-hill where it is thrown and, in token that this has been done, a little cruse, with lighted wick, is placed upon the rubbish heap. Then, the home is lighted up. Scores of dips, in little earthen platters, are lit along the walls of the courtyard and the home. Presumably, the significance of this procedure is that as the righteous Ram purged Ajodhia of all its dross, so should the individual cleanse his home of all the litter and rubbish which has collected during the year.

Another legend has sprung up through the Ages, in connection with *Diwali.* In the long, long ago there lived a mighty king, the Raja Nal. As he reclined upon his sofa, he called to a courtier and commanded that he should play him in a game of chance. The bashful courtier made excuse that there were no dice to be had. Raja Nal burst into a passion at so poor a plea and, unsheathing his sword, severed his own thighbone, flinging it to the courtier with the command "No dice in all my kingdom! Take this, and from the bones make me the dice I want." The dice were made and the game was played. Half the kingdom of Raja Nal was the stake. The courtier won. The shock of defeat, even more than the decapitation of his leg, resulted in the death of Raja Nal, whose body was thrown into the river. The bones of that body have made all the shells and *cowries* which are yielded up to-day by sea and river alike and thus, these substitutes for dice are used to the present day. Since then, the receptacle for the stakes, the pool, is known in Hindi as the 'nal' and the subject, like the courtier, gambles on *Diwali* night to enrich himself and to propitiate the ancient Raja Nal.

Perhaps, it is with the crystallisation of this belief that the festival has come to be associated with Lakhshmi, the Goddess of Wealth. It is in the hope that Lakhshmi will smile upon her devotee and grant him a free ticket to the get-rich-quick estate, that gambling is universally indulged in by the Hindu at *Diwali* time, almost as a religious rite. Thus, also, the festival is sometimes called *Dip Malika*, the latter word having a possessory significance.

Philologically, the word *Diwali* is of more than usual interest. The most common interpretation is that the word is *Dipvali*. Where *dip* means exactly the same in Hindi as in English *viz.*, a wick dipped in wax or oil, and *vali* is a contortion of *mala*, a ring or wreath. Thus, *Diwali* would mean " Wreath of Light" ; but the correspondence of the English and Hindi word *dip*, together with the unsatisfactory connection between *vali* and *mala* almost indicate that the western root "valere" in French, suggesting "value", would be more appropriate. Reasoning *a posteriori* from the fact that the Goddess of Wealth is worshipped at this time, we are led to the irresistible conclusion that this is almost a more acceptable theory.

Howsoever that may be, what of it? *Diwali* is the festival of light and of joy, of good cheer and of abandon, of gambling and of wealth, of *lawa* and of *batashas*, of toys of mud and toys of sugar, of feasts and of fairs. India is happier for it. Little else matters.

III.—*Muharram* : Its Significance and Importance.

Muharram is that season of the year when all Islam mourns the death of their martyr-saint, Husain and the *tazias*, representing his coffin, are reverently laid to rest. It is then, that the *Muharram* drums beat out their funeral dirge and many a *majlis* and *maulud* is held. The *majlis* and *maulud* ceremonies are services at which the praises of Hussain and Muhammad are recited, couplet by couplet. As each couplet is recited, the gathered assembly expresses itself in heartfelt chorus, sometimes of pain and lamentation, sometimes of praise and adoration. As the story of the fateful battle of Karbala is recounted, their hearts fill with fervour. And now, the reciter refers, in the couplet, to the scorching effect of the merciless rays of the sun on Husain who stands, falchion in hand, facing his foes, with blood streaming down his face. Some of the listening audience cry out in agonised expression, others shed silent tears. The recital finished, a short prayer follows in the form of a benediction. Then, certain stalwarts come forward and beat their chests in a wild staccato, measuring their time with the oft-repeated words, *Hasan*, *Husain*. The same thing is then repeated with iron chains which have triangular spikes at their ends. Each terrible blow of self-inflicted injury causes blood to gush out, and some of the performers fall with the severity of the strokes.

One wields a sword, and with every repetition of the words *Hasan, Husain*, he cuts himself on the forehead, till his whole face is streaming with blood. So, proceeds the agonising of the Moslem soul over what is to him the most terrible tragedy in history, where a martyr saved to the world the religion of Islam by accepting the potion of pain and death. To understand the significance of the festival it is necessary to recount the whole sad history of the event.

Many centuries ago, Yazid, the grandson of the leader of the infidels, demanded homage from the saintly Imam Husain. It was refused; Imam Husain, replied that he bowed his head to no one but the one God who was the Almighty. Forthwith, Yazid sent out his hordes to subdue Imam Husain, who by then, was proceeding to Kosfa, called by the people of that place to come and ameliorate their condition after the excesses of the tyrant, Yazid. Imam Husain and his followers lost their way in the desert and encamped at the fateful Karbala. There, their path was intercepted by 32,000 men under the leadership of Shimr, a captain appointed by Yazid. From the 1st to the 7th of the month of *Muharram*, the Imam begged of the opposing force to desist from violence. He prayed that unnecessary warfare and bloodshed should not be entered upon, but to no avail. All his reasoning, all his pleadings, all his persuasion fell upon deaf ears, and on the 8th day of *Muharram*, Imam Husain realised that all was in vain. A desperate struggle must ensue, he must be overwhelmed by superior numbers—in a word, he and his party must suffer massacre, for the fiat of the unbending Yazid had gone forth by then, that nothing but the severed head of Imam Husain would satisfy him. So, Imam Husain prayed for the postponement of the inevitable battle till the following day. His prayer was granted. That night, while all the camp-fires were twinkling around him in that desert camp, he gathered his followers around him and addressed them in a long and heart-appealing speech. He warned them of the coming horrors of the following day, he told them of the sure massacre to ensue, he emphasised that all those who stayed by him were doomed to martyrdom, and then he performed a beautiful act—so full of consideration for human weaknesses, so pregnant of the spirit of sacrifice, so indicative of the kindness of a great heart. He had all the lights of the camp extinguished and as he did so, he told his followers that those of them who had not the courage or the heart to stand the coming martyrdom, might depart unknown and unashamed in the darkness which now befell the camp. In the morning, as the clusters of purple clouds began to gather on the Eastern sky, there stood 71 faithful followers around the Imam, resigned to the death of martyrs. Imam Husain, armed with a flashing falchion, mounted his pure white charger, *Zuljinah*. The enemy came out strong and powerful, and the opposing forces—so disproportionate in numbers—clashed in mortal combat. One by one, the Imam's followers went down fighting, overwhelmed by superior numbers. Hour by hour the sanguinary struggle proceeded. The Eastern sun rose up higher and higher and cast its rays, with relentless force, on to the blood-soaked plain. Imam Husain's party were parched with thirst. His son—still but a child—asked for water and the Imam lifted him into the saddle, picked up a leathern bag *mashak* and, slowly but steadily, fought his way up to the river bank, dealing deadly destruction on every side as he advanced. At last, the river bank was won. He lowered his *mashak* and brought it up filled with cool, sparkling water. As he raised it to the lips of his son, an arrow came upon its flight and piercing through the *mashak*, buried itself into the heart of his son. The *mashak* emptied itself; his son shuddered and died in his arms, and the sorely-tried Imam returned into the thick of the fighting with new strength and fresh vigour, slaying all who came within reach of his sword. The field of battle was filled with dead and dying. His helpers were all killed. Closely pressed on all sides, at last, his faithful charger was felled with a heavy sword-cut. Riderless but undaunted, the Imam carried on the desperate struggle, wielding death-dealing blows on every side, till he was overcome, wounded and killed. It was then midday, and the scorching sun was high in the heavens as it looked down on the glazed eyes of the martyred warrior, fixed in death. So died Imam Husain, a defender of the Faith. Worse followed. His children were killed and his wife was taken prisoner and carried off by the victorious enemy.

It is the memory of this glorious history of warrior martyrdom that the festival of *Muharram* perpetuates. Is it surprising that the faithful follower, the firm believer, is stirred to tears at a memory so great and grand? Is it surprising that strong feelings assert themselves, that militant passions are aroused, that a religious fervour plays upon the heart-strings of every true Musalman? Is it surprising that, when they carry the *tazia* which represents the coffin of the sainted Imam Husain, tears well up in their eyes? When the drummer beats with all his fury on the great *Muharram* drum which reverberates enough to burst itself and fills the earth with echoes of thunder-claps, he sees all these scenes of one-time battle passing before his eyes with kaleidoscopic rapidity. When the sharp rat-tat of the cross-sticks is heard, when flashing sabres are wielded round with lightning rapidity, the minds of the performers go back to Karbala, back to the blood-stained desert, back to the hard-pressed Imam, and they are filled with feelings of mingled fury and sadness and religious zeal. Is it any wonder then, that these people, to whom religion is life and life is religion, with so glorious, so stirring a history to bring to mind, should rent their hair and beat their chests in lamentation and cry out, in their agonised distress, "O! Husain!" That is all they can do these many centuries after, in respectful memory of their martyred saint. Helpless to help him, but not helpless to honour him, to let their hearts beat in sympathy, they beat their breasts and cry, "O! Husain," and again, "O! Husain", and again, a hundred times, "O! Husain."

This is *Muharram!*

THE GANGES.

(Written on the occasion of the great "Kumbh Mela" at Allahabad in 1930.)

Great *Ganga* from *Gangotri's* giddy height
Bursts into life and rushes down,
With giant might and silvery light,
Down, through gorge and valley, down—
    And the silent hills, they watch her go,
    Speeding on and on for evermore.

Here cataract, there roaring waterfall,
Leaps down to kiss the foam below,
Enmantled in a gauzy pall
Of spray with multi-coloured glow—
    And the stately pines, they watch her go,
    Speeding on and on for evermore.

Through the foot-hills, now she winds her course,
In the lower valleys of the "Doon,"
Through the gorges, with increasing force,
Hissing her familiar tune—
    And the proud Siwaliks watch her go,
    Speeding on and on for evermore.

Now Hurdwar's reached: in front, the plains;
Great *Ganga* moves magnificent along:
The temple-bells ring out, and myriad swains
Offer her praise in prayer and song—
    The hermit and the martyr watch her go,
    Speeding on and on for evermore.

Past Saharanpur, she grandly glides ;
Then, on to proud Farrukhabad ;
Swelling as the ocean with incoming tides,
Shedding on the Hindu soul her **asirbad*—
  And the smiling fields, they see her go,
  Speeding on and on for evermore.

Along her banks, rise forts and monuments,
Vain structures of the human hand !
And myriad palaces and tenements,
Here glittering, there crumbling in the sand—
  With reverent eye, they see her steady flow,
  Speeding on and on for evermore.

And now, the voice of commerce meets the ear,
The clatter of a thousand factories,
Against the sky a host of chimneys rear
Their heads, with horrid buzz, and wheeze—
  And Cawnpore's trade and merchants see her go,
  Speeding on and on for evermore.

Onward, then a hundred miles she rolls,
As if impatient now to greet
Fair Allahabad, where countless Hindu souls
Await her where the rivers meet—
  The colleges and temples see her go,
  Speeding on and on for evermore.

---

* *Asirbad*=Blessing.

'Tis here the Jumna, like a damsel fair,
Enswaythed in robes of deepest blue,
Moves slowly on and adds her share
To her sister stream of sombre hue—
    The millions at the *_Sangam_ see her go,
    Speeding on and on for evermore.

'Tis here the Saraswati hides,
Like bashful maid behind the veil,
To meet, with subterranean tides,
Her mother's waters grey and pale—
    With triune sanctity, we see her go
    Speeding on and on for evermore.

Roll on, thou emblem of divinity,
And give thy peace to those who wait
On thee with faith and certainty,
And find in thee a heavenly gate—
    Roll on, with sacred and eternal flow,
    Speeding on and on for evermore.

---

* 'The _Sangam_' = The place of confluence of the three rivers, considered the most sacred and purifying by Hindu bathers.

The late R H Niblett I S O , M A , J P , whose stories of the "Ol Faithfuls are recounted in these pages

OLD FAITHFULS.

A True Story of India Half-a-Century Ago.

I.—Parauti and the *Indian Banshee.*

"GHOSTS! Nonsense! I am not superstitious." Nor am I, and I have said this myself more than once. But here is a story which had material results of unmistakable significance. It is not an experience of my own, but it is one for which I can vouch because it was told me by one whose veracity I could trust more than that of anyone else in the world—my father. He was a man with an excellent sense of humour and a better power of telling a good yarn; but when he had finished, he always made it clear if the story he told had no basis in fact. This was a tale, however, which he related to me in all seriousness and the truth of which he absolutely vouchsafed.

It is many years now, but I can remember clearly that summer evening when the old man, with his grey head and serious countenance, told me the story, in slow deliberate tones. As near as I can remember, this is what he said:—

"It was in 1886 that I was transferred from Rae Bareilly to Sultanpore. To-day, we have trains which clatter over these parts and would convey you that distance within the course of a few hours. But in those days, the journey was a formidable one, and had to be performed by slow-moving stage-coaches with many perils along the way. I, of course, had my own horses and my dog-cart, so I was independent of the ordinary stage-coach. My arrangements complete—a horse at every stage—I commenced my journey. Something delayed me at the start, but as it was a crisp winter day, I did not mind commencing my journey shortly after midday. I remember it was my beautiful mare "Stella," who started me on my journey. At the next stage, 8 miles away, I changed horses and now, I was being taken along at a slow jog-trot by old Obedah whose days of work were really numbered. And then, at the next stage, I harnessed fiery *Shaitan* who was my favourite riding-pony and who strongly resented being made a cart-horse. But once started, he sped along like the wind, finishing his 8-mile trip in 40 minutes by my watch. He finished so fresh, neighing to his relief along the roadside, that I almost regretted I had not doubled his distance. It was now about 4 o'clock and I had my afternoon tea here in camp-fashion while the horses were being changed. The new animal was a sturdy *bhutia* pony I had named "Barney." He stepped out well, but his little stride did not exactly furnish speed for it was after 5 o'clock that I reached my next stage. The sun was already looking like a great redolent globe of light on the horizon. Before me lay miles and miles of long white road now looking grey in the evening light. There were two more stages to go and only one of the two horses along the way had any pretensions to speed. I was now driving poor old 'Juno' who was really getting past work and who I was retaining more as a pet than as a working proposition. I tried to urge the old lady on; but it was no good. She kept to her steady, measured pace, mile on mile. The road was bordered on both sides with an interminable row of trees—old banian trees, hoary *pipals*, majestic *nims* and towering mango trees—which threw ever longer and darker shadows along te road.

To-day, the marauding *Thags* of India are a memory of the past; in those days, they were a very real menace of the Indian road. Many poor wayfarers, through those wild *jungle* expanses, suffered at their hands and were left dead upon the highway with no witness but the silent trees and the lonely road to see and to preserve their secret in the hollow chambers of their muteness.

It was not exactly fear: it was a lively apprehension which laid hold of me as I drove on and on in my high-seated district cart with its great iron-bound wheels rumbling and ever rumbling till my ears tingled with that sonorous buzzing refrain punctuated by the constant tap-tap-tap of the iron-clad hooves of Juno's steady pace. Suddenly, an owl would shriek out into the silent night with ear-piercing cry and then another, as if to soothe, would deliver its mournful, deep-voiced hoot with lulling hollowness. And then, silence again, save for the rumble of my wheels and the staccato of Juno's hoofs.

"*Sahib,*" said a deep voice behind me, "if you will stop a minute I'll light the candles of the carriage-lamps." It was my old syce, Parauti, who was my only human companion on the journey. I reined up. What silence! The rumbling had ceased, but in that silence, somewhere in my imagination, I could still hear far far in the distance a faint rumbling. My ear, somehow, could not shake off the symphony which it had heard for so long. Can it be some other journeying person, I asked myself, and I strained my ears to listen. But no, it was not. It was difficult to convince myself that it was not, so used had my ear got to the sound. Meanwhile, old Parauti had deftly and silently, leapt off the footboard at the back and was lighting the candles. The matches were the old red-tipped Tanderstickers which burnt so long with blue flame before bursting into yellowed light. Silently, Parauti did his work but silently as he did it, every little sound he made echoed from the hollow bowl of space around us. The very snap of the lamp-clips, as he closed them, sounded like the distant crack of a gun—so intense was the silence. As he turned to go back to his seat, suddenly, in the distance, I caught the sound of a faint faint cry. It was the cry of a woman—a woman in distress. "Listen!" I said to Parauti. "Listen, it is some woman crying." Even in that half-light, I could see a look of terror come into Parauti's eyes as they flashed out their message of superstition and fear. "It must be a *Churail*, *Sahib*. Drive on, *Sahib*. Drive fast. Let us flee from her. It were better that we came face to face with the *Thags* than with a *Churail*. Drive faster, *Sahib*." "Don't be a fool, Parauti!", I replied, "There is no such thing as a ghost—male or female. What is more, we seem to be getting nearer the sound for I can now hear it above the rumbling of the cart, so it hardly helps you if I drive faster." The tremble which went through Parauti's frame was communicated to the lightly-built cart and I could perceptibly feel it even as we jogged along. "*Sahib*," he said in half-choking voice, "in your country there may be no *Churails*, but in India they are very common. My father was killed by one. O, *Sahib*, believe me that I speak the truth." "Don't talk nonsense, Parauti!" I said, "Some silly idiot told you your father was killed by one and you believed it. It's all utter rubbish." Parauti was silent. I think he must have been praying. The cry became more defined. Clearer and clearer it came, but in the gathering darkness, I could discern no object. Now, it seemed right by the roadside. And then I saw an object—just a shadow under the over-hanging branches of a low *pipal* tree. I drew up. "*Sahib, Sahib,* for God's sake, don't stop," begged Parauti, "It's a *Churail, Sahib.* I swear on God, it's a *Churail.*" "Keep your silly tongue still," I said sharply, "I must question this old woman." In the dingy glow of my candle-lamp on the near side of the road, I could see her—an old decrepit hag with deep lines of age across her face. Sycorax was not in it! She rose wearily to her feet and all humped and huddled, moved slowly towards the cart. Juno, who was usually as steady as a rock, veered away from the approaching apparition; but I steadied her. Parauti, who was never slow to respond to the call of duty, was cowering in a veritable tornado of fear at the back of the cart and never attempted to hold Juno. However, I realised his feelings and controlled the mare. "What are you doing here?" I asked the old woman. With whining voice, she commenced her tale of woe. "My son," she said, "is dying in Sultanpore and I made an attempt to reach him but was benighted on the way. I am an old woman and cannot walk much at a stretch. I cry because I know not whether I shall see him alive to-morrow when I reach." "Poor thing", I thought, "Surely I could help the old woman by giving her a lift on my trap," "Come on," I said, "I'll see you to Sultanpore." Then, turning to Parauti, I ordered him to help her on to the back of the cart where there was plenty of room for two.

"Villainous hag! *Churail!*" cried Parauti, "Would you deceive my *Sahib?*" and then turning to me he begged as I have never known a man to plead for life itself. "*Sahib,* I beg you, I beg you, for Mercy's sake: in the name of my only son, I beg you not to take this woman. She is a *Churail* and some dreadful misfortune will overtake us."

His excitement seemed so foolish that I lost all patience. "Look here, Parauti," I said "I've had enough of this, you hard-hearted brute. For the sake of a silly superstition, you wish to leave this poor old woman here with a breaking heart. Obey my order at once and help her up. Parauti was as a man struck dumb. Torn between superstitious fear and a desire to obey as he was wont to do at all times, he seemed to sway where he stood. Before he could act, the old woman had laid trembling hold of the edge of the trap and with amazing litheness, had scrambled up. Parauti seated himself at the very edge of the other side, his eyes peering out like blazing balls of fire, terror-stricken and almost distraught with fear. Seeing them both seated, I looked to my front again and drove on. It was only another mile to go and once or twice, I glanced back and saw that my human freight was safely ensconced at the back and Parauti's eyes were still fixed, still flashing fear, as I drove on. Soon, I could see a camp-fire in the distance and in front of that pale radiance, a horse was silhouetted. It was my next stage, and with some impatience, I urged Juno on. Soon we were there, and I reined in. Parauti delayed a little in coming forward. "Parauti!" I called, "Hurry up, it's getting late. Have you got so fond of the old lady that you don't wish to——". I glanced back and as I did so, Parauti jumped off, but I could see no signs of the old woman. At that moment I was filled with the most consuming rage. 'Scoundrel!" I cried, as I leapt off the cart and made towards Parauti, fully intending to beat him soundly in spite of his age, "Blackguard! You have knocked the old woman off on the way." Parauti fell at my feet. His words melted my heart and made me control my temper. "Master, master," cried the venerable old man, "I have served you so long. I would give my life for you. My body is yours to beat. My life is yours to take. I swear before God that I never knocked the old woman off. She suddenly disappeared as we drew near this camp-fire. She just vanished into the air. I was so surprised myself, that I was looking in amazement where she sat when the cart stopped. *Sahib*, believe your faithful servant, she was a *Churail*, a dangerous, damnable *Churail* and this has proved it." I could not but notice the earnestness with which Parauti spoke. He was decidedly not lying consciously. I presumed, however, that what had happened was that the old woman had fallen off herself on the way, and Parauti, with his weak eyes, had not noticed it in the darkness. Harnessing my fresh horse, Cæsar, I decided to drive back to the spot where I had last seen the old woman seated securely at the back. It was only a mile and we covered the distance quickly but there was not a sign of the old woman. Then, like the sigh of the night-wind, I could hear a wail in the deep shadows of the forest to the northern flank of the road. With remarkable rapidity the voice came nearer and nearer. In a moment, from the brushwood, a lone jackal suddenly broke, and slouched past. From the spot, almost immediately after, emerged the old woman, waddling along in doubled-up and crouched attitude. Cæsar, who had let the jackal pass unmoved, now snorted and backed. He was a spirited animal, and Parauti ran up and held him. The old woman, still crying, commenced to repeat her story all over again in plaintive and whining voice. "I've heard all that once", I said, "and I have no time to go over it again. It's getting late. Jump up now. When I reach my destination, you shall tell me how you fell off and if it was my syce who had something to do with it, I shall deal with him adequately there." The old woman did not seem to understand what I was talking about, but I took it that she was too old to grasp things quickly, and possibly demented as well, both with senility and with fears for her son's life. Once again, the old woman scrambled up with surprising alacrity. "Now, let the horse go Parauti, and come on," I said. "Protector of the Poor," pleaded Parauti, "Let me sit at your feet, but not at the back with that *Churail*. If some misfortune should befall us, if this *Churail* should kill me, I wish to die with my head at your feet." "Parauti, sit at the back as I have ordered you," I commanded, "and if that old woman should fall off again, I shall be certain that it is no accident but deliberate rascality on your part. It is now nearly 8 o'clock and I am too tired to sit and talk nonsense to you." Parauti, hesitated a moment. "Sit down!" I thundered and I started off. Parauti was all but left behind. With a spring which would have done credit to a younger man, he leapt on to the footboard at the back and sat on the edge of it, glaring at the old woman. I drove on. Cæsar was a splendid young waler and covered ground at a tremendous pace. It was the last lap of my journey and I thought hungrily of dinner. The furlong posts seemed to pass with kaleidoscopic rapidity, and then in the distance, I saw the lights of Sultanpore. What a thrill went through me! The tiredness the journey had wrought seemed to lift itself. Cæsar stepping high, with arched neck and strained nerves, was pressing onwards at a magnificent rate. I looked round now and again to see that all was well with my antagonistic passengers. Both of them were sitting facing each other and now I noticed the old woman had opened her eyes wide and was staring wildly at Parauti. Parauti was glaring back at her. There was something, however, in the old woman's eyes which I did not like. They were distinctly evil, but I took it that it was natural annoyance with one who had abused her and, possibly also, knocked her off. In front, was a long dark avenue and my dingy lights made me peer into the vista lest I should meet a camel-cart or bullock-cart on the way, so near to civilisation. Once again, I looked back and saw the old woman and Parauti seated behind. But it was only a glance as my attention was focussed ahead. Hardly had I turned, when I felt a sudden jerk as if a weight had come off from the back of the trap. I heard a blood-curdling cry—then a heavy thud. Cæsar leapt forward in frenzied manner and I pulled him in with all my strength, stopping him within a few paces. I seemed to be too stunned with the suddenness of the incident to realise what had happened. At first, it seemed to me that half the cart had fallen away. As I looked back, I found the cart was all right, but no one was on the footboard at the back.

And then, I heard a deep groan from a huddled-up figure on the road. I ran to Cæsar's head and turning him round, brought him up to the figure. The dim light now fell upon it: it was Parauti. I went a few paces further back, leading Cæsar, but could find no signs of the old woman. I returned to Parauti. He was speaking in short, sharp jerks and almost inaudibly. Still holding Cæsar's reins, I knelt down by his side, with one hand on his shoulder, to listen. He slowly stretched out his hand and drew my foot to his head and then very gently, in a choking whispered voice, halting with each word, said "Master, I die happy because I die with my head at your feet. I know—I—am—dying. It—was the same—*Churail* who—killed my father. She threw me off—and—disappeared. *Master, Sahib*, I leave my son—to you. His—mother died long ago. Promise me—my *Sahib*—that you will be both father—and mother—to him." The last words were so faint I could hardly hear them and before I could speak, before I could clear the lump in my throat, Parauti's eyes closed. I thought he had passed away, but to confirm the trust reposed in me, I said, "Parauti, depend on your *Sahib*. Your son will be safe. Poor Parauti! You were right." Just then Parauti opened his eyes again and looked straight into mine as if he understood, and then they glazed in death, still fixed upon me."

* * *

My father paused and for a full minute there was unbroken silence as he seemed to be gazing into the star-spangled sky of that summer evening. And then, as he rose to go, he added, "I have kept my promise. Soman, your bearer is Parauti's son."

II.—A True Story of the Loyalty of old-time Indian Servants—Nohri *Chamar*.

He is an old, old man now, bent and decrepit in appearance, hobbling along with the aid of a stick and hardly able to see a foot before him. He is my pensioned bearer, Nohri.

My earliest recollection of Nohri is of a man, pugilistic in frame, carrying over his shoulder a woman with her throat cut, streaming with blood. That was over three decades ago, when I was hardly out of my infancy. It was many years after that, I asked my father to tell me the details of that blood-curdling sight with which my child-mind was so deeply impressed. My father commenced in slow measured accents to give me the history of Nohri and how matters led up to the incident.

"It was long before you were born or even thought of," said my venerable old father, "that I was out camping in my magisterial capacity in the Azamgarh district. The advance tents to my next camp had been delayed in transit owing to the darkness of the night and the absence of a well-defined road. The result was that I arrived at my new camp to find all was not ready for me and the last tent was just being pitched. With nothing else to do for the moment, I sat and watched the pitching of the tent. It was a tent something after the Swiss Cottage type ,and my camp followers were assisted by enforced labour in the form of *chamars* from the neighbouring village. My old orderly, Karamat, who was doing the least work, was spending his time abusing these poor ill-fed, half-clothed, low-caste labourers who were gloriously willing workers, but equally as gloriously ignorant of what a tent was or how it should be pitched. Soon, the tent was up and the little band of ignorant *chamars* slunk away like jackals from the scene. A young man amongst them lingered a little and then, with very hesitant manner, said to Karamat "*Do paisa mil jae?*" ("Could I get 2 pice?"). Karamat turned on him savagely. "Cheat!" he yelled "One would think it was not enough honour done to you, son of a pig and eater of pigs, that you were privileged to put up the tent of the lord of this *Tahsil* and now you dare to ask for payment. Begone! or I shall break every bone in your body. The old autocrat was shaking with resentment and was distinctly insulted at so insolent a request. The young *chamar* smiled apologetically and folding his hands, stood on one leg as a sign of humility, begging to be forgiven for the offence he had given. "Don't stand there like a vulture then," snapped Karamat, "Be off, don't you see the *Sahib Bahadur* is sitting there?" The young man, looking wistfully in my direction, slunk away. I watched the whole proceeding interestedly and then, as the man was moving off, I said "Karamat, call that man to me." "*Huzur*" said *Karamat* smartly, as he called to the man thus, "Here, you low-bred carcase-eater, come back here. The *Sahib* wants you." And he added confidentially, "You presumptuous knave! I told you to clear off. Now, you shall get your leather taken off you for your insolence." The young man, with a look of terror in his eyes, trembling with apprehension, approached in suppliant attitude. "Mercy, mercy, *Sahib*," he cried in the coarsest accents, "I have sinned. Forgive me. I shall never do it again." He would not give me a chance to speak, so importunate was he in begging forgiveness. "Shut up," shouted Karamat, "Stop braying like a donkey." The man stood on one leg, with folded hands and looked as if he was going to receive sentence of death. "What is it you want ?" I asked as kindly as I could.

"I—I only want forgiveness, King of the World. Forgive me", he bleated. "No, no," I said rather impatiently, "What did you want from the *chaprasi* ? " "I am a jungly man, Protector of the Poor, I am a fool. Forgive me. I foolishly asked for two pice", he wailed, "I'll never do it again. Forgive me, judge of all men."

"Karamat," I said, "Give him two annas from my account. You certainly should pay these poor devils who help in pitching tents."

Karamat's face fell. "Very well, *Huzur*; but oh ! my father, my father, this will thoroughly spoil the custom, *Sahib*, and these miserable low-caste insects of the earth will completely lose their heads. Forgive me, *Huzur*, for presuming to warn your noble self of this impending danger."

"Don't argue," I said sternly. "Pay him and let him go and, in future, you will pay all such helpers in my presence."

Meekly, Karamat obeyed, and the young man *salamed* deeply. He was just moving off when I said, "Wait, I want to talk to you. What is your name ? " "Nohri," he said hesitatingly. "How old are you ? " I asked.

"I am about twelve years of age," he said innocently. "Idiot ! " snapped Karamat from behind me. "*You* are twelve years of age ! What an enormous ass you are. You cannot tell the truth and say you are about twenty-five. Liar ! "

"Karamat," I said gently reproving him, "Let me talk to this man and don't interfere."

"So you say you are about twelve years of age?" I said reassuringly, knowing twenty-five was a correct estimate. "No, *Malik*" he replied quickly, "I must be twenty-five. The *Chaprasi Sahib* says I am twenty-five."

"Have you any brothers?" I asked.

"Yes! *Malik*, one."

"How old is he?"

"He must be 50 or 60, because he is older than I am."

I gave up talking of ages as I realised figures conveyed no meaning to him.

"Are you married?" I asked.

"Yes! *Malik*."

"Have you any children?"

"Yes! *Malik*, two sons and four daughters."

"What?" I exclaimed in surprise, "You have six children!"

"Yes! *Malik*" said Nohri "You see it is this way. My father was a very poor man and could not afford to get me married till a very late age." He seemed to think my surprise was that he had not got *more* than six children!

Just then my *khidmatgar* announced breakfast and I dismissed Nohri and went into my tent.

I was three days at that camp and every day, I saw Nohri somewhere on the borders of the grove. As soon as he saw my eyes on him, he would slink away lest I should be annoyed. The time now came to move to the next camp and Nohri was back again, helping to unpitch the tents. As I was riding off, Nohri came running after me and I could hear Karamat's angry voice shouting after him, "Come back here, insolent knave. Come back, presumptuous worm." Nohri, however, was determined to risk everything, and running up alongside of my horse, prostrated himself on the ground. "*Malik, Malik,*" he pleaded, "let me go with your camp. I want to serve you." "But in what capacity can I take you?" I said, "I have got my permanent staff of personal servants and need no others."

"I shall pitch your tents at every camp, *Sahib.* Only give me enough for one meal a day. Let me come," he pleaded. The request was so earnest, I could not resist it.

"Very well," I replied, "You may come."

At the next camp, Nohri was there, furiously busy. He seemed to walk with an air of importance now, and even tried to tell the *chamars* at the next camp how many sorts of fools they were and how ignorant each of them was in the matter of pitching tents. Was he not the permanent *pro tem kuli* of the Lord of the *Pargana!*

The winter months passed, and with them, the days for touring. Finally, at the end of March, just as the harvest was ripening and high winds had commenced to blow, the last camp was reached. The next move was to headquarters and just as I was preparing to go, Nohri ran up to me with very sad and distressed face. "Well, Nohri," I said, "You must go back to your village and next December when I start touring again I shall appoint you a camp follower once more." I could see a real tear glisten in his eye as I spoke. "O! Protector of the Poor. Let me come to headquarters with you. I'll do *any* form of work you want—anything, on any wage. Don't turn me out, *Malik.*"

It was then, a thought struck me—and I said, "Wait, let me see—I shall need a *punkha-kuli* (fan-puller) in a few days, so go home now, and come to me at Azamgarh on the 1st April", and I chuckled to myself to think how suitable the day was to the appointee. Nohri's face brightened up. "Very good, *Malik*. Very good," he said, "I shall come."

At dawn on the 1st of April, my dog barked furiously and persistently at something at the gate. I sent Karamat to see what it was. I did not need Karamat to return to know what it really was, "This is the worst of you miserable low-breeds", he was shrieking in a high-pitched voice. "The idea, the cheek of you arriving at this time of the morning and disturbing the sleep of the *Sahib Bahadur*. A little bit of encouragement and you low-born scoundrels get thoroughly spoilt and out of hand. And, then, like a *Nawab* you needs must enter by the front gate——" And so he kept on haggling like a splenetic old woman.

I called out in stentorian voice, "Karamat! Is it Nohri? Let him come." "*Huzur*," came back Karamat's respectful reply in disgusted tones.

In a moment, Nohri arrived accompanied by Karamat. A row of white teeth, peeping out from a darkly-bronzed face, told of the joy and pride with which he had come to take up his new post.

He was dressed only in a loin-cloth and over his shoulder, was a small piece of bamboo from which was suspended a dirty-looking bundle about the size of a water-melon. This was all the worldly property he carried. The bundle contained a brightly-polished brass vessel which Nohri had inherited from his father and the rest was ground gram or what he called *sattu*.

"How on earth did you arrive so early?" I said, "Your village must be 26 miles from here."

"I started last evening," said Nohri, "Just as the sun was going down."

"But weren't you afraid of *thags* on the way?" I queried.

"No, *Malik*," he replied with a look of amusement on his face, "Why should *thags* want to waylay me? I am a poor man, and had nothing which could be useful to them."

I rose to go inside to dress and as I went, I told Karamat to instruct Nohri how the fan was to be pulled. I thought it would be interesting to watch the lesson through the chink in the door.

Karamat gripped the rope and gently pulled and released it in regular sweeping motion, while Nohri watched him, greatly amused. "What are you grinning for; you insolent knave?" snapped Karamat. Nohri's countenance became immediately somnolent. "Here, take," said Karamat handing the string over.

No Viceroy of India seized the reins of authority with greater pride and enthusiasm than Nohri grasped at that rope. "Now, pull," said Karamat. I saw the muscles harden up on Nohri's shoulder and thighs. Shutting his eyes, he gave one almighty jerk to the rope: the connecting cane smashed and Nohri went backwards, rolling on the ground, holding up in his hand the rope attached to the broken piece of cane. The annoyance, the disgust of Karamat at that moment is beyond description. With utter contempt, he exclaimed, "May your soul burn in hell-fire, you miserable idiot! Do you imagine you are hauling a *dol* (leathern bucket) out of a well? You coarsened *Chamars* do not understand the delicate nature of tasks assigned to a servant in the house of an English *Sahib.*" Nohri scrambled to his feet rather badly bruised, but terror was written in his eyes as he looked at the broken cane in his hand. "*Dohai* (mercy) *Chaprasi Sahib,*" he cried, "I have committed an unpardonable fault." "Rapscallion !" cried Karamat, "The price of six canes will be deducted from your pay at the end of the month and one of these broken pieces I shall keep to flay your hide for you next time you commit such a fault."

A new cane was then brought and fixed. Nohri caught the rope gently and tremblingly, drew it with the utmost caution. And soon the lesson was learnt. I came out to find the *punkha* swinging away, Nohri sitting in the *baramdah,* steadily pulling.

Nohri had been assiduously performing his duty for a whole week when one day, I heard him whisper to Karamat who sat at the door, "*Chaprasi Sahib,* I see something moving inside." Old Karamat was in a doze, and woke up with a start. "Something moving ! Where ?" he asked. "Is it a stray dog that has got in ?"

"No, no," said Nohri, "It is moving in the air. I think it is a ghost."

"But where ?" said Karamat, "I don't see it at all."

"There, there, *Chaprasi Sahib,*" said Nohri with increasing excitement, "It comes and goes every now and then."

And Nohri pointed to the end of the *punkha* frill as it came into sight every time he pulled the rope.

Karamat turned on him with contempt, "*That* ! That's the *punkha,* you fool. You have been a week in the *Sahib's* service, but you continue the same. Can a *Chamar ever* get civilised ? Go on with your work and don't talk again."

Gradually, the summer passed with its long long hot days and the monsoon burst, and that season too swung past with its insects and depression and humidity. On the 1st of October I had to relieve Nohri of his fan-pulling duties and tell him to go home. But no ! he was determined to be kept on. He begged on bended knees not to be dismissed. Once again, I fell to his pleading and I allowed him to stay on as a general help to the bearer. He would clean my shoes till they glistened and he looked upon lamps with a keen and scientific eye, considering their mechanism absolutely wonderful.

A year later, I was transferred, but Nohri would not leave me. He insisted that he would stay on in my service for the rest of his days. So he came with me.

For years, he followed me from posting to posting."

My father paused to light a cigar and then continued, " Well, it was about seven years after Nohri came into my service that I was married and then you children came into my life. Nohri was more gentle with you as babies than a woman could be and so I appointed him as full bearer to look after you."

" But what about the murderous incident you were going to tell me about ?" I asked eagerly.

' I am coming to that," said my father. "Let me take you through Nohri's history, step by step.—Well, you were only two years of age when Nohri, who had cared for you so tenderly, was one day, filled with a desire to see his own children again.

"'May I have ten days' leave and go home, *Sahib*?' he asked. 'Well, ten days' leave after ten years' service is not an extravagant claim,' I thought. 'Yes! certainly', I said, and a far-away look came into Nohri's eyes as he conjured visions of his little thatched home far away and his loved ones waiting for his return. 'I had a dream last night, *Sahib*,' he said 'that my family is in trouble. I left them two *bighas* of land but as they were only tenants-at-will they could be ejected at any time by the *Zamindar* and I wonder if this forbodes evil.'

"'Yes! if you feel like that, go by all means,' I said. His eyes now gleamed with joy as he said, 'My boys must be quite big now. May I bring my eldest son with me, *Sahib*? Give him some work in your own establishment and he will serve you as I have done.'

"'Very well, Nohri. Bring him along', I assented. Here, my father's voice just seemed to choke a little, but he continued. 'A new hope seemed to spring up in Nohri's heart. He had put away Rs. 36 during his service and this to him was a great fortune. He commenced to purchase presents for the various members of his family. Before he left he brought and showed them to me with great pride. There was a steel trunk for Re. 1-8 and two brass vessels for Re. 1-13-9 which he had haggled for and bought for his wife. There were four *saris* (dress cloths) for his daughters and two brass-bound sticks for his sons. With all these extravagant(?) purchases, his capital had come down to Rs. 29-7-9 but he waited for pay-day and, taking his Rs. 5-8, he prepared to leave. Trains were now running to Azamgarh, and Nohri had worked it out in his mind how he would pay Re. 1-9-3 for his fare and after the purchase of some sweetmeats for his children and some good rice for the home, he would have something over Rs. 30 to spend on the weddings of at least two of his daughters which he was determined to arrange during the course of the ten days he was on leave.'

"At last, the moment for his departure arrived and he bid us all a respectful goodbye and went. I watched him go. From the bungalow, his room in the servants' quarters was plainly visible. He put on the old pair of ammunition boots I gave him a year before, he donned an old overcoat which I had presented to him two years after he came to me. Under his arm, he carried an umbrella which was an acquisition in which he took especial pride. Along with the umbrella were the two brass-bound sticks for his sons, and on his shoulder, the steel trunk containing the *saris* and brass vessels.

"And so, Nohri, with merry heart and buoyant stride, stepped out of the *compound*, to the Railway Station."

* * *

Again, my father paused and looked intently into the fine smoke which went curling upwards from his cigar.

I was just about to ask him again, "But what about the incident?" when he continued, very slowly:—

"You," he said, "were a very little fellow then and I remember that nothing could console you when you discovered that Nohri had gone. Anyhow, even to your mother and myself, the house looked different. Something seemed missing and that something was Nohri.

"However, two days passed and late in the evening of the third day, as I was sitting out in the *baramdah* an apparition appeared before me, and then it sank down on the ground and held my feet. I could hardly realise what it was and yet, in that twilight, I could discern a familiar face for the momentary period that the apparition stared at me before it fell at my feet. It was Nohri. He was dressed as I saw him first, ten years before, in a loin-cloth all bespattered with mud that had dried upon it. His cheeks were hollowed. His eyes were deeply sunk and staring. He could not speak. And then, a low moan came from his huddled body as he gripped my feet tighter. Suddenly, he found his voice and the moan became a cry as he said, '*Sahib*, I have lost everything—everything—but you.' I was amazed. 'Could this wreck be Nohri?' I asked myself. 'He who had gone out so happily in the full health and vigour of a young man only three days ago?' '*Whatever* has happened?' I asked in alarm, 'Tell me. Calm yourself, and tell me.'

Nohri began. '*Sahib*,' he said, 'as I was approaching my village trying to catch a sight of my old home, I met the *Zamindar*. He could not recognise me when I *salamed* him and asked me who I was. 'I am Nohri,' I replied, 'don't you know?' 'Nohri! Nohri *chamar*!' he said, 'and you dare to come into the village precincts with boots on your feet and an umbrella over your head and an English coat on your body? Have you forgotten your origin; that you belong to the lowest of the low and that you insult my dignity by coming in this garb into my village?' On saying this, *Sahib*, he ordered his men to snatch away all I had, leaving me in this loin-cloth. He then had me beaten, and you will see the lacerated wounds on my back. Then, he sent me into the fields to work—not because the work was necessary, *Sahib*—but because he said he wanted me to realise my position and from what stock I came.

"'But, surely, he returned your things to you later?' I asked.

"'No, *Sahib*, he did not, but I did not want them back either. Listen to me, *Sahib*. Listen to my tale of woe to the end.'

Nohri continued, 'It was midnight, *Sahib*, before I was taken, under escort of the *Zamindar's* servants, to the *zilla* where the *Zamindar* lives. There, I was ordered to be put into a room for the night. And all the time, I was longing to see my home and my wife and children again. I could not sleep and the desire to be free, overpowered me. I decided to try and escape. Gradually, I lifted the thatched roof and after hours of effort, I slipped out unnoticed. It was then dawn and how changed my village looked. I hastened to my home, but there, to my horror, I saw only a ruin. I went then to my brother, Jagat, to enquire from him where my family had gone. Jagat had grown grey and could not recognise me. He was delighted when he found who I was. I was impatient to find my family. 'Jagat,' I said, 'where is my *prani* (soul) and where are my children? I see the old home is in ruins.' Jagat looked surprised, and then said, 'Have something to eat and I shall tell you.' But I was impatient and I said, 'I cannot eat, I cannot think. I must know where I can find them.' Then, I seemed to drift into a dream as I could hear Jagat's voice speaking. 'Your family,' he said, 'have lifted their tents and gone to Parmeshar long long ago. Shortly after you left, the *Zamindar* demanded that your wife should become his mistress and when she refused he took away her tenancy. I fed them for some time and your wife continued to look forward eagerly to your return. Then, she got the impression that you were dead, and one day in a fit of despondency, she jumped into a well with her two youngest children. Before we could get them out, they were all dead. Then plague swept the village the following year and the remainder of your children——.'

Nohri's voice broke. He could not finish the sentence; but I felt his whole frame shaking beneath me.

"Nohri was never the same man again. The merry twinkle in his eye had gone. He was usually grave as he went through his daily tasks. He seemed, after that, to enjoy placing himself in danger. If there was a snake to kill, Nohri dashed forward to slay it with a *lathi*. If in camp, a hyena laughed its hideous laugh into the night air, Nohri was out on the war-path to meet it. If a mad dog darted into the compound, Nohri was after it with any sort of implement he could pick up. He seemed to care not a bit for his life, and to thoroughly enjoy taking risks."

* * *

My father paused again and lit another cigar. Then he went on rather more rapidly than he had hitherto done.

"At that time our *bhisti* (water bearer) was a man named Barkat: a powerfully built young fellow, with a goat-beard, blood-shot eyes and a pretty little wife in *purdah*. This girl came over to the bungalow one day to see your mother who was astonished at her delicate loveliness. She could not have been more than 15 years of age, said she was of Mogul descent, and had great sweeping eyelashes and a light olive complexion. Barkat was most jealous of her, but he made it a daily habit of beating her unmercifully over the most trivial domestic occurrences. Sometimes, it was because his food was burnt, at other times, because it was not cooked enough, and at yet other times, when it was not cooked to time. The poor girl—hardly out of her childhood—was most unhappy. Imprisoned within four walls, with nothing to do but to cook food and await the return of her lord and master, Barkat, she lived in her lonely solitariness through the dull routine of life. The out-office which Barkat occupied was the only double-storeyed one in the compound and his little wife spent her days in the upper storey—the lower one being kept by Barkat for the entertainment of his friends.

"It was a hot June day that you children were playing in the back garden under the superintendence of your bearers, Nohri and Soman. Hearing your shrieks of delight, Barkat's wife partially opened her attic window to look at the game which was in full swing. Barkat happened to pass that way and suddenly his eyes fell in that direction. He frowned angrily as he caught a glimpse of his wife behind the half-closed window. At that moment, dark thoughts clouded his vision. He assumed, at once, that his wife was attempting to attract the attention of these two young bearers, and he planned his revenge.

"It was just as we had sat down to dinner that we heard the cry of a woman's voice coming from the direction of Barkat's house. 'There's that devil Barkat beating his wife again', I said. 'Probably his dinner is not ready.' Soon, the cries became more insistent and tumultuous. Then, there were shrieks which rang out with guttural sound. In a moment, Nohri hurried into the room, saying in wild excitement, '*Sahib, Sahib!* Barkat is murdering his wife. There he is at his window.' I sprang to my feet and ran out, shouting for a lantern with which we hurried to the spot. There, in that dingy light, we could see Barkat holding his wife's hair with one hand and with the other, drawing a table knife slowly and deliberately backwards and forwards across her neck. She was struggling ineffectually, with both her delicate hands, to push aside the strong right arm of her husband as it was carrying out its murderous task. On Barkat's face was a broad, diabolical smile. His lips were murmuring, '*For this offence I should really cut off your nose, but I prefer to* start lower down.'

'Let her go, you scoundrel', I shouted. 'Let her go. I command you to let her go.'

"'When my deed is done' said Barkat. 'I shall let her go and I shall hand myself up to you. You can hang me after that, I care not.' And all the time the knife kept flashing backwards and forwards till the woman's voice became more guttural and faint. Soman was hurling himself at the lower door to get access to the upper room and suddenly, I saw a ladder go up under the attic and Nohri was nimbly climbing up, unarmed. 'Come nearer and I shall plant this knife into your neck,' Barkat yelled at him. Nothing daunted, Nohri climbed on and, like a flash, he had grasped Barkat's hand and twisted it with tremendous force. The knife, still held in Barkat's hand, was now pointing upwards streaming with blood. 'Jump on my shoulder,' Nohri cried to the woman. 'Quick!' As she jumped, Barkat fell with her, and Nohri, still grasping his wrist with a grip like death, slung him aside with furious force. He fell senseless to the ground below in a pool of blood and Nohri descended with the unfortunate woman on his shoulder.

"'Take her to the *memsahib*,' I ordered. 'Soman, run along as fast as you can go and call the doctor.'"

* * *

Once again, my father paused for a moment. Then he continued :—

"That was the time you saw this sight. Well! the doctor came, but the woman was unconscious by then. He shook his head and said 'Little hope ; but one never knows.'

"'Now, doctor,' I said, 'will you come and see the murderer?' He lay where he had fallen. He was dead.

"To our surprise the woman lived, but she was only able to speak in whispers ever after.

"And that's all there is in the story" said my father as he got up from his easy chair. "He's a splendid fellow—Nohri."

* * *

It was many years after this that a funeral procession passed along the road. It was my father's. Far behind the long line of mourners, a little band of decrepit servants, the old faithfuls, followed. There was Ramzan Khan, the grandest of them all, bordering on 90 years of age, who had carried my father in his arms. There was little old Ganga, a grass-cutter, who had risen to the rank of syce, and there was Nohri—good old Nohri. In every eye glistened a tear.

A decade and more has passed since then and after many years of absence from Allahabad, I returned and saw old Nohri. He was sitting on a stone slab on which he was assiduously scratching at something with head bent low. I approached him silently and looked over his shoulder while he was unconscious of my presence. On the slab was written, Nohri *Sirdar*. "What are you up to?" I asked. The old man looked up with a start and said, "*Baba*, I know your voice. You are Lancee *Baba*." He touched my feet and gripped my arm fervently in both his hands. "Yes! you're right", I said, as Nohri tried to strain his dimmed old eyes to look into my face and see me, "But what are you doing with this slab?"

"Oh! *Baba*," he said, still addressing me as he did in the long-ago when I was a child, "I am making my gravestone. My time has come and I want to be buried at my old master's feet." It would have been cruel to disillusion him as to the impossibility of burying him in a Christian graveyard. "As I was with him in life, so I wish to be with him in death," said the old man fervently. "Every night, I smell his cigar near my house and I know that his spirit is with me."

"But you are a Hindu, Nohri" I argued. "You cannot be buried. You must be cremated and made over to Mother Ganges in the end."

"*Baba*," said the old man, his eyes brimming with tears. "I know not Mother Ganges. I had one god. He was your father. Bury me at his feet. Promise me, *Baba*. This will be the last wish of your old bearer. Promise me", he pleaded.

I passed it off. "Don't talk about death, Nohri," I said, "You'll live to a hundred yet. So there is lots of time to arrange things. Here's a rupee. Now, have a jolly good drink and make up your mind to outbeat me in the race of life."

I patted the old man on the back and came away.

* * *

To those who are sceptical let me say, old Nohri is not a myth. He is to-day in Allahabad; and in the out-offices of a house on Cawnpore Road you will find him, sitting on his slab, preparing to meet his master and his "god"—the only god he knows.

III. RAMZAN  KHAN

[Of the splendid 'old faithfuls' who have served my family in India, the grandest of them all was Ramzan Khan. There is no memorial I can erect adequate to his memory. There are no words which could bespeak eloquently enough the gloriousness of his devotion. There is no loyalty which could surpass his. There is no service I have seen which was more devoted, more self-sacrificing, purer, grander than that of Ramzan Khan. In illness or in health, he stood staunch to his post. With fever wracking his bones, at 90 years of age, we had to quarrel with him because he refused to go home and take to his bed. His is a memory which can never be forgotten by any member of my family. His life was a sermon to others who would serve. It was more; it was a sermon to his masters. To me, personally, his memory is a golden link that chains me in bonds of love for India for ever. As a humble tribute to his glorious memory I have attempted to indite this little poem which, however, touches only on the fringe of Ramzan Khan's great and devoted services to my grandfather, the late Philip Niblett, J.P., and the generations which followed him.]

Five and seventy years ago, in our good old Hindustan,
Lived a dashing Indian soldier—a handsome young Pathan.
He rode his horse with pride as he galloped with his lance.
With its pennant flowing free and his arm at full advance.
Splendid trooper! Ramzan Khan.

In stature he was small, but his body was erect,
As he trotted to parade in his uniform bedeck'd;
There was fire in his eye and a down upon his chin,
With his *pugri** neatly tied o'er his bronzed and ruddy skin.
Good old warrior! Ramzan Khan.

Then, there came the fateful year of 'Eighteen-fifty-seven'
With its Mutiny, and oh! 'twas Hell where there was Heav'n!
Disaffection spread around: the disturbers of the peace
Spread a canard that the Army was supplied with lard as grease;
He also heard it, did Ramzan Khan.

The rumour spread like wild-fire: the troops were in revolt;
They massacred their Officers; 'twas like a thunderbolt!
They looted all they could and they ravaged every town,
And their war-cry it was "Down! with the curs'd *Firingi*,† down!"
'Twas otherwise with Ramzan Khan.

* *Pugri*=Head-dress.
† *Firingi*=Foreigner.

He sprang upon his charger and galloped to the Mess
To defend his British leaders 'gainst mutinous excess.
But alas! before he reached, the deed it had been done,
The floor was strewn with corpses; the mutineers had run.
He wept—did Ramzan Khan.

Then, he made for Civil Lines to speak about the crime
To warn the Europeans of the danger of the time.
'Twas then he hotly rode to the lonely bungalow
Of the English Treas'ry Off'cer and told his tale of woe.
"Flee, *Sahib*, flee," said Ramzan Khan.

"I'll go with you," he said—he was looking deathly ill—
"My own beloved *Sahibs* are lying stark and still;
"Oh! *Sahib*, let me save you and your children from this Hell,
As a token of devotion to the *Sa'bs* I've loved so well,"
Said the gallant Ramzan Khan.

As he spoke, there came a noise of bedlam on the road,
A shrieking of the mob, as they near and nearer strode.
"They're coming in their hundreds, they're beating at the gate,
"Flee, *Sahib*, flee—before it is too late,"
Hoarsely whispered Ramzan Khan.

Without a moment to be lost or a minute to prepare,
The family of five—their faces drawn with care—
Rushed distraught through the house and left it from the back,
Each parent held a child, and as for little Jack,
He followed, in the arms of Ramzan Khan.

Unnoticed, now they sped, with the bungalow between
The mutineers and them, till they gained the far ravine,
Through that long secluded valley, they trudged along apace
Till the shadows of the evening closed on India's sunny face.
"Rest, *Sahib*, now," said Ramzan Khan.

Before the breaking of the dawn, they were on the march again,
Till they reached the Grand Trunk Road and a wild deserted plain,
There, they found a broken culvert, with a hollowed cave inside,
'Twas a haven for the footsore and the weary to abide.
He left them there, did Ramzan Khan.

Through the hot and dreary day, they could hear, at intervals,
The rumbling bullock-carts and the tinkling of their bells;
Then, a cavalcade of rebels came clattering on their way,
Crying thirstily, "*Firingi*" *—All India was at bay!
But not so—Ramzan Khan.

As the darkness gathered round, they heard a steady pace
Approaching every moment, their secret hiding-place:
The anxious parents' eyes fill'd with horror and with fear,
"We're discovered! We're betrayed!" They prayed for Heav'n to hear,
But it was only Ramzan Khan.

* *Firingi*=Foreigner.

He brought them two *chapatis,** his face was full of care,
"This was all I could procure, *Sa'b*, forgive the humble fare."
For sixty-seven days, the family remained
In that subterranean home, praying, hoping and sustained
By the care of Ramzan Khan.

The Mutiny suppressed and peace again restored,
The family emerged, but the babe that they adored
Had gone where babies go, to the Fairyland of God,
Its body laid to rest and covered with the sod,
By the gentle hands of Ramzan Khan.

From that troublous dreadful time, for seventy years and more,
He served the family—through generations four.
His beard turn'd snowy-white, his body bent and frail:
Through the rolling years of Time, loyalty the "Grail"
Of the faithful Ramzan Khan.

A year or two ago, he went to see his home,
In a little village town with many a mosque and dome,
One night, he fell asleep: "in Christ" it must have been:
His—the purest, whitest soul that India's ever seen.
He's now in Heav'n—is Ramzan Khan.

* *Chapatis*=Indian cakes.

The Shah Sahib.

An Indian Village Mystery.

IT was in January, 1927, that into the quiet Indian countryside there walked, with steady and solemn tread, a Mohammedan mendicant—a Shah Sahib. He was dressed in a long flowing green robe that matched the burnt sienna of the dusty road and the emerald hue of the fields that stretched out on every side. His eyes were a rich hazel in colour and extraordinarily mild, while now and again a peculiarly juvenile twinkle seemed to play over them. His beard was grizzled and spoke of fifty summers or more, but his face was singularly free of wrinkles and there was a ruddy glow under the light brown of his cheeks. Altogether, he looked a picturesque sight as he walked steadily on and on with swinging motion and easy gait through the fields and the *dhak jungle* and past little hamlets snugly ensconced in groves of leafy mango and *pipal* trees. And, every now and then, his eyes looked upwards seemingly for spiritual guidance as he hummed a religious refrain. It was thus that he entered the village of Ara Kalan in the Allahabad district. The dust of the road had settled on his clothes and beard and added rather than detracted from the picturesque appearance he presented. Here, at Ara Kalan, over the tops of the little thatched huts and humble homes of the peasants, he could see, towering upwards, the minaret of a ruined mosque. Thither he wended his way. Better to rest in a ruined house of Allah than in a palace meant for human residence! Hot and weary he arrived and then, made his way to the ruined well to wash his feet and prepare to say his evening prayer. The sun was already sinking on the western horizon, and in another ten minutes the time was to arrive when the faithful follower would cry out his evening *azan* and lament before God for the sins of the day.

A village girl at the well had just finished drawing her pitcher of water for the evening meal, and as she prepared to go, the venerable Shah Sahib arrived. She drew her cloth across her delicate features no sooner was she aware of the presence of the saintly Shah Sahib. Though only a girl of sixteen, she was a widow who was married in childhood and had actually never set eyes on her husband, thus even in the presence of a reverend personality like the Shah Sahib she felt embarrassed. "Daughter!" said the old man "Give me some of the water you have drawn. I have no rope to draw with." Immediately, the water was supplied in the Shah Sahib's vessel and Qutubunnisa *Bibi* hurried away to her home where she lived with her old father-in-law Nadir, a *Jolaha* (or weaver) by caste. "Father" she said as she arrived out of breath, "there is a *Fakir* at the mosque and he asked me to give him some water which I did. He must have no food either. Shall I cook some and will you present it to him in the name of Allah?" "Let me go and see him" said Nadir, and away he went to the mosque, but before he reached, he could hear the Shah Sahib's voice plaintively crying out the evening *azan* calling the Faithful to prayer.

For years the *azan* had ceased to be called in distant Ara Kalan, the mosque had been allowed to go into ruins, spirituality had waned and now, as the evening air rang with that soulful and melodious refrain, the followers of *Islam*, heart-stricken and touched, hurried to the spot to see whose voice it was that had filled all their souls with fervent joy and spiritual appeal. There, they saw the saintly *Islam*, standing humbly before his Maker crying out his heart. Slowly and reverently, they moved up to Nadir, who had arrived before them, and the gathered company stood themselves silently behind the Shah Sahib, who now ceased his crying and proceeded to pray in silence, groaning deeply now and again in an agony of spiritual supplication. Sometimes he would kneel, sometimes he would stand and at yet other times he would prostrate himself on the cold, bare ground as his spirit wrestled in prayer. The village Moslems who stood behind him emulated his every movement and their souls were filled with a spiritual calm and with gladness. And then the prayer was over. The old Shah Sahib turned and faced them without the least surprise. "O, followers of the True Faith!" he said, "Fie for shame! To think that you have so far ceased to fear God or to regard His holy commandments that you have ceased to pray, that you have allowed this house of prayer, this mosque, to go into ruins. But it is not too late. I come as a messenger from God to tell you that this mosque will be replaced by one which will come down upon it from heaven, as the bird comes down from the sky and rests upon a branch. Only have faith. Do as I tell you, and continue to pray, also play incessantly on a tom-tom day and night and collect alms for the poor. I shall stay here within these sacred precincts for a day and then I shall move into one of your houses which must be vacated for me. The house must be emptied of all earthly goods and the door must be locked. On no conditions, must that lock be opened for thirty days within which time, if it be God's will, a heavenly mosque will come down upon the site of this ruin you have here. Go now and leave me to agonise in prayer for the day of the fulfilment of this promise which God has whispered in my heart." Mystified, amazed and filled with religious zeal and fervent prayerfulness, the gathered company bowed deeply to this prophet of God and departed unto their homes. Then, Nadir returned and asked the Shah Sahib to take his evening meal at his place and return after it to the mosque.

Qutubunnisa *Bibi* had worked hard and by the time her father and the Shah Sahib arrived, she was ready with a dinner as rich as their poor circumstances would permit. She served it herself and the Shah Sahib, tired after his long journey, and hungry after his long fast through the day, ate heartily of the repast and retired to the mosque.

Next day, the Shah Sahib returned to Nadir's house and the news of his prophecy having reached far and wide, a great crowd of Hindus and Mohammedans gathered to see him. He addressed them all, repeating what he had said before and asking the Hindus also not to be distrustful but to believe in the event to come. Having finished his sermon, he pointed ominously to the door of the house next to Nadir's saying, "Into that room now, I shall go and serve my self-immolation. Have it cleared of all it contains. There must be nothing worldly to withdraw my attention from things eternal. The room must be absolutely bare." "But what about your food, Shah Sahib?" asked Nadir anxiously, "May we make a trap-door and slip food into you each day?" "Alas," said the Shah Sahib "do you think I care about food when I am receiving heavenly succour? I shall ascend within that room and like a spirit, rise out of it. When next you see me, you will notice me standing at the threshold of the new mosque, coming down from heaven."

The house ordered to be vacated, belonged to Ahsan. He felt privileged at the selection and hastily cleared the room. Qutubunnisa *Bibi*, who was watching from the door with awe-filled eyes, was touched to the depths, and gathering up a little straw, threw it into the house in case the Shah Sahib wanted something more than the bare ground for a bed.

And now, the moment of the highest thrill had arrived. The Shah Sahib stepped firmly towards the door, his head bent low. As he entered, he turned to Nadir and said "You, I appoint an earthly representative of mine in my absence. You are to sit by the tom-tom day and night and see that it is played incessantly. Each day at sundown, you are to say a prayer and send the money collected into your house to your daughter-in-law, who will guard the money as her very life. It will bring a curse on any one who dares touch or steal that money, for it is God's." And then, the doors were closed on the Shah Sahib.

Day and night the tom-toms played their steady staccato tune and people from all the neighbouring villages gathered. Alms, from both Hindus and Mohammedans, poured in. Each day, the collection became larger. Those who did not have money to give, offered their jewels. And each evening, the faithful Nadir said his prayer and deposited the collection with Qutubunnisa *Bibi*. The amount became so large that a look of fear came into the eyes of pretty little Qutubunnisa *Bibi* as she was seen carrying away the amount

But there was one sceptic amongst the people. He was he village *Zamindar*, a *Thakur*. He was extremely annoyed at the continual noise of the drumming which made sleep impossible and life unbearable. Apart from this, sometimes in his more credulous moments, bigotry got hold of him and it struck him that if a mosque did come down from heaven, it would be an advantage to Mohammedans only and the Hindus who were subscribing their all would either be unable to use this place of worship or be converted to *Islam*. After three weeks, the music still continued to play and no voice could be heard within the locked door through which the Shah Sahib had passed. The irate *Zamindar* appealed to the authorities about it. The *Tahsildar* Magistrate tried to persuade the people to cease the playing of music, but to no effect. Their religious zeal had attained a pitch of fanaticism, and interference meant trouble. So, the *Zamindar* was asked to let the period of thirty days pass.

The thirtieth day arrived and the whole countryside gathered from far and wide to witness the great miracle. Day passed and night came. Through the freezing atmosphere, the expectant crowd sat by little camp-fires waiting with their eyes fixed on the mosque. Midnight and morning came and Nadir was looked upon with suspicion. The people commenced to ask for a return of their money. They demanded that the house of the Shah Sahib's incarceration be opened. Nadir begged that this should be done before the authorities and he suggested that they may have misunderstood the number of days mentioned by the Shah Sahib.

Within a few hours, the Sub-Divisional Magistrate with he Station Officer of Police and a party of constables arrived.

The key was asked for, but Nadir said he had lost it. The lock was broken open and the doors thrown apart. There lay the cold bare room, empty save for the few wisps of straw that Qutubunnisa *Bibi* had thrown in before the Shah Sahib had entered. Someone trod on the straw which lay in the corner, and down sank his foot. The straw was removed and revealed a hole going down at a slant. On being excavated just a little, the mystery was solved, at least partially. The hole led into the house of Nadir. Qutubunnisa had the key of Nadir's house but Qutubunnisa could not be found and has not been found to this day: nor has the Shah Sahib: nor the money.

Nadir was in tears; but obviously he was not in a position to enlighten anyone. He had followed the Shah Sahib's commands strictly and made over the money to Qutubunnisa *Bibi*, never leaving his post to come inside his house.

The Mosque from heaven has not yet descended. Perhaps it will, when the Shah Sahib and Qutubunnisa *Bibi* return!

[This story is based on fact, and it is not meant to imply that the person styling himself a "Shah Sahib" was, in fact, one, or for the matter of that, a Mohammedan.]

A Visit to the *Dargah* of Saiyad Salar Masaud at Bahraich.

It was in the sacred month of Ramzan,
Sacred to every true Musalman,
That I ventured out to this shrine to go
When the *loo* of the day had ceased to blow,
As the calm of a summer's evening fell
On the silent tomb with a soulful spell,
While the golden spire beat back its gold
To the setting sun o'er the distant wold,
And the silver'd dome caught the dazzling light
And changed its hue to a reddening white,
While the crystal glint of the minarets
Gleamed out in the sky like flaming jets.

It is the tomb of Salar Masaud,
The resting place of his bier and his shroud,
And here to this mausoleum's side
Come crowds that gather from far and wide.
Moslem and Hindu in long pilgrimage,
The flippant, the fervent, the seer, and the sage.
With padded footsteps I softly tread
The smooth marbled surface that lay ahead
On every side stood the fretted walls
Of the cool and carvéd marble halls.
Here, the tomb of the Saiyad Masaud
Of regal birth, from the Kings of Oudh,

O'er the grave was spread a gold-edged pall
While fragrant roses were strewn o'er all.
Nearby to the martyr's buried corse
Lay buried his standard, his dog and horse.
Not these alone, for near him is laid
Fair Zohra *Bibi*, the devotee maid
Who sought this sanctum in centuries past;
On its curative power her trust she cast;
Here her blinded eyes received their sight,
Here she stayed till her gladdend soul took flight
And clung to the soul of the sainted seer
In the realm of the spirit, unseen, somewhere!

And yearly the crowds that here repair
Marry this saint to this damsel fair;
When with reverent hands this tomb is laved,
With hands which perfected love has enslaved,
The water that flows off its sloping sides
Drifts out to a pool and there abides
For the sick and the lame, the halt and the blind
To immerse themselves and remedy find
For their palsied limbs and torturing pain.
Bethsaida's power revealed again!
It is the sanctum of Salar Masaud
A martyred saint and a Musalman proud.

Here rests his body and excalibur
He died in the faith, *Allah-ho-Akbar*!
As silent I went, so silent I go
With thoughts uplifted and head bent low

At the gateway there kneels deep sunk in prayer,
A lonely *khadim*, with stony stare
There, clad in pure white, his soul uplifts
As, nearer to God it gently drifts.
Long may the tomb of Salar Masaud
Preserve the sweet calm with which 'tis endowed.
The peace of the shrine shed rest on my soul,
As I wished it adieu and homewards I stole.

[*N.B.*—Near this *Dargah* is a fathomless pool called Anarkali and the local legend is that, in the long ago, a golden boat used to rise up from that pool. The boat contained gilded plates bearing food for the poor. One day, a poverty-stricken person after partaking of his meal, stole the empty plate. From that time the boat never emerged again and it is believed that it still rests at the bottom of this unfathomable pool. It is further alleged that some people, within living memory, have seen—or imagined they have seen—on moonlit nights, a phantom boat riding along the smooth surface of the pool.]

AN IDEAL OF INDIAN WOMANHOOD

Plates by kind permission of
The Fine Art Cottage
Allahabad

Kamala: The Ideal Hindu Wife.

THE Indian love-ideal of *Laila*, the idol of *Majnun*, is almost surpassed by the conception of Kamala. In the former we have a damsel of surpassing loveliness attracting her wooers by sheer force of her beauty. In the latter we have a devoted wife who is consumed by the madness of love for her husband—the one and only man who occupies the whole of her mental and spiritual horizon. We have no description of Kamala, but we are left to glean her character from her wonderful whole-souled passionate "letters to her husband," Krishna. She sits in solitary loneliness, "in the sanctity of self-abnegation" pouring out Love's fragrance with her pen in unhesitating freedom of speech. And then the madness of her love begets dreams of jealousy and in the train of those dreams comes jealousy—imagined and unreasonable—jealousy itself—then tragedy. She loses the pen her husband gave her as an emblem of his love, she loses her pet parrot which has been to her a constant companion behind the veil, and the lowering clouds of madness gather round her sad life, and realising the deadly grip of that terrible mania as it slowly takes hold of her, she cries out in an agony of soul to her husband: "Do come. Do come, before I am completely gone and it is too late." Then comes a letter, at last, from her husband, but in a half-hearted strain—a letter towards which she had looked so long and eagerly. This completes the ruin and in resignation, she writes: "The happy time we spent together—oh! it was all a delusion, a dream from which I now awake! I fancied I was your prisoner. You have now set me free and I am at large like my pet. I pray Thee, O God, take me away this instant! take me into Thy holy presence, for I am free from all earthly bonds and the task Thou did'st allot to me in this life is done." Here we have the ideal conception of a Hindu wife's duty. It is entirely towards her husband, her liege and her lord. When he needs her no more, "the task Thou did'st allot to me in this life is done."

Then follows the last heart-rending letter, the final call and the last farewell. Here we have a quaint and beautiful representation of the clasp of death, of a "Messenger,"—"a big strong man with a beard, a beautiful net in his hands which he is unfolding and getting ready for me." As the folds of that 'net' gradually draw round her and she is smothered in their loving embrace, still Krishna is her last thought—more than earth, more than everything else. "Goodbye earth and everything" she cries. "Goodbye Krishna! I am gone—gone for ever!"

To the modern materialistic mind, all this looks like the ravings of a lunatic, but that is exactly what it is, though of a lunatic distraught by the power of love. To some it will look like the acute sufferings of a neurotic, but that it is, though of a slave of love—the whole-souled love of a Hindu wife. It is an ideal of the East and consequently the Westerner must try to look at it with the vision of the East to appreciate it to the full. In the West, the feminine ideal is almost invariably the unfledged maiden; here, the ideal is of devoted wifehood. The idealism of the East then commences where the idealism of the West ends.

Kamala is not the ideal of Rider Haggard. For example, she is not selfish like the heroine of " Mr. Meeson's Will." She is not self-willed like Beatrice.

She is jealous, but she is not jealous like Juno who turned her daughter Io into a heifer because Jupiter fell in love with her. Nor does she evade her lover like Daphne, who turned into a laurel tree when pursued by Apollo. So the idealism of Mythology does not apply to her.

No heroine of Shakespeare, either, is like her exactly. Shakespeare's ladies are all high-born, displaying delicate honour, rapidity of decision, quickness of sympathy and absolute trust in instinct. Kamala does not pretend to be all this. She is merely a household ideal—but a very beautiful one at that. She possesses something of the ethereal quality of Miranda—completely unsophisticated, absolutely simple—compact of the very elements of womanhood, but her character is brought out in stronger relief by the display of a towering jealousy. She possesses something of the character of Rosalind in the sweet vacancy of the forest of Arden, but she is capable of assimilating more of the few worldly observations which lie along her narrow worldly path. She philosophises when she sees a cat and says that, though the omen be bad, she must call the cat a friend for giving hei timely warning of her own sin and fate. Then, again, take her rhyming observation—

" A housewife fair is a husband's foe,
A husband rich is the housewife's woe."

This smacks of the philosophy of Portia, but there is an entire absence of pedantry in her philosophy. She is the direct antithesis of the rude and stubborn Cordelia. Like Ophelia, she goes mad, but the reason for Ophelia's madness remains a mystery. In the case of Kamala, it is clearly the imagined faithlessness of her husband. Her dreams make her, like Hermia and Helena, the sport of fairics, but unlike Hermia and Helena she does not become a slave to the fairies themselves. She presents the dazzlingly white and saintly figure of Isabella in 'Measure for Measure,' but her character is entirely uncompromising with wrong and she could not, like Isabella, plead the cause of guilty love even for a brother. She has the sensitive affection of Desdemona and the proud sincerity of Cordelia, but without the other little foibles present in these characters.

Kamala is a character by herself. Kamala is Love and Love is Kamala. She is a personification of the perfect love and devotion of the perfect wife. It may be argued that her consuming jealousy mars the perfection of her love, but without that strong jealousy the overwhelming devotion she professes would become unreal. That jealousy is a necessary concomitant of her love. It brings out all the real fire of the character of Kamala until she burns like a flame in the sky of Hindu sentimental thought. Those who have read Kamala's letters will realise that the general impression that there is no real love behind the veil is utterly false.

The Song of the *Durmut.*

(1)

There's an instrument, the *durmut,* with which they beat
the roads,
It's a relic of old India and its engineering modes,
It's a simple wooden staff with an iron weight below,
With which they crush the *kunkar,* singing gaily
"*Maro! Ho!*"

Drap! Drap! Drap!
A hundred *durmuts* go,
The *kunkar's* beaten down
With each united blow,
Drap! Drap! Drap!
It comes in measured beat,
Like tramp of marching men,
Like myriad marching feet.

(2)

A host of ragged coolies in solid phalanx stand
Each wielding his own *durmut*—a mud-bespattered band!
In unison they beat, oh! how perfect is the time
Of this wild staccato music, of its metre and its rhyme.

Drap! Drap! Drap! etc.

(3)

Let old India move along, upon her speeding way,
Let politics advance and her customs pass away,
But there's still an ancient link that binds us to the past
The manner of the metalling that time has failed to blast.

Drap! Drap! Drap! etc.

(4)

Sometimes I think of India, which my early boyhood knew,
Of Lachan and his wife on the cart the camel drew,
And now I see their children in motor-lorries squashed,
Another link is broken, but all is not yet lost.
Drap! Drap! Drap! etc.

(5)

I'll be sad the day I see, the roller worked by steam
Displace the ancient *durmut*, with its horrid engine-scream,
Still I'll listen for the echo of that steady thumping sound,
When I hear it in my fancy, sweetest mem'ries will abound.
Drap! Drap! Drap! etc.

Dâk Bungalows of India.

ENSCONCED in the deep shadows of a well-wooded grove, it stands—the Dâk Bungalow. In front, the long, long white road which stretches for many hundreds of miles and passes scores of similar retreats. As the midnight motorist flashes past he gets a glimpse of these time-worn walls looming up out of the darkness of its surroundings. There they stand like silent ghostly sentinels, as they have stood for decades past. In the day, when the rays of the summer's sun are pouring down relentlessly on the thirsty wayfarer, whose eyes are burning with the *loo* and whose throat is caked with hot dust, how attractive this sanctuary of rest looks. How its cool shade and shelter calls the wearied traveller, till instinctively he obeys the behests of that inner calling. All is quiet, save for the crickets which creak with incessant lulling sound in the trees and occasionally the owl in the leafless *pipal* hoots out his mellow mournful song—deep and low, deep and low it comes and it speaks of summer. We reach the bungalow. All is wrapped in a mantle of silence. We go round it, and at the back is a small row of servants' quarters. One of the doors is half open and from it comes a steady burbling sound with occasional pauses in between. It is the ancient *Khansama*—bearded and old and bent, drawing lazily at his hobble-bobble. We call. He comes out immediately with *salaming* obeisance. Back he goes, but only for a minute, and he emerges again with a rusty key at which he blows furiously at intervals, evidently with the intention of cleaning it thereby. He throws the doors of the bungalow open and we enter a musty atmosphere, but pleasant withal. Every article of furniture is caked with dust, but this does not detract from the appreciation of this veritable oasis in a desert of dust. A bat scrambles out of the hiatus in the ceiling and narrowly misses ricochetting off our heads. On one table lies the Visitors' Book—ragged and yellow and torn. We turn the pages and it is like looking on a scroll of the dead. Names of those long since retired and dead; names of those who had in the year of entry noted their designation as 'Joint Magistrates' and now are High Court Judges and members of the Board of Revenue; names of world tourists who succeeded and those whose efforts ended in disaster. With what different feelings these visitors must have visited this bungalow. There are those who came here on cold inspection duty, those who hated the loneliness and whose only pleasure was the imaginary tinkle each day of Travelling Allowance dropping into their pockets, five big tinkles and then a smaller one. The days T. A. was earned. Little else mattered. Then there were those who came here for a rest in the countryside. They had eyes to see and ears to hear and they both saw and heard. They saw the gnarled *jamun* tree to the east which had formed the sport of the *chhokra* boy half a century ago and was still the happy hunting ground for the village children to seek and to find fallen fruit. Then there is the banian tree—so shady and cool and inviting. How many a happy honeymooning couple had sat in that shaded bower and whispered words of love and confidence undisturbed by the stare of a scandalising world. Towards the gate, bordering the rutted road, stands the majestic avenue of melantolias with their soft leaves waving in the breeze and their little fluted blossoms, some pink, some lily-white, dancing above in the sunlight or leaving the branch and fluttering down to kiss the brick-red earth below. To the west, a row of *pipal* trees—some half a century old, others but saplings. How restful must these be to the Hindu eye as he conjures up, in his imagination, the myriad gods which sit upon the leaves on Thursday afternoons. Upon the topmost branch, sits a vulture brooding in silence. Yonder a bamboo clump, its long stalks waving gently in the wayward breeze. A slight rustle of leaves and then again a hush. Under it, in a secluded corner, sits a maniac hermit. He is older than the *Khansama* himself. He looks up unconcernedly at me and then pokes at the little fire before him between four bricks. I ask him how long he has been there. "Fifty or sixty years" he says, and then with a long quizzical look he adds, "This country is all changed. We do not have *Sahibs* as we used to have. There was Nicholson *Sahib*. He earned *four hundred* rupees a month." He said "four hundred" with that emphasis that one would imagine he was mentioning the total value of all the precious gems contained in the Tower of London. He went on. "But Nicholson *Sahib* was a real *Sahib*. He could abuse better in our language than any Indian and his voice was like thunder." He stopped abruptly and after a moment's pause he queried "What is your pay?" "Six hundred" I replied. He looked at me aghast and long, and then he gave a sceptical smile. "Six hundred," he said "then you must be the Collector *Sahib*?" I assured him I held no such high office. "Six hundred" he repeated, and then with a little sceptical laugh, he said "I saw you walking on your feet to-day to the village. Six hundred rupees! Why, Nicholson *Sahib* used to go there on a caparisoned elephant with a red and gold umbrella over him. H'm! six hundred rupees!" His voice almost developed a sneer. But he went on talking, "Why, I remember once, when I was acting as footman to the *Raja* of Majhauli, we saw Nicholson *Sahib* coming on horseback and the *Raja Sahib* stopped his four-in-hand and got out of the carriage to say *salam*." This old mendicant is Sher Ali, a retired servant of the Majhauli *Raj*. He asserts he is 100 years of age and I do not think he is far wrong. He remembers the time when the present coachhouse of the Dâk Bungalow was raised to its now enormous height and he cannot understand why motor-cars are so low and so silent. To him there is no grandeur in any vehicle which is neither high nor noisy! His knowledge of money is antiquated to a degree, and as he receives charity in kind and not in cash, he does not know the depreciation in the purchasing power of the rupee. In another ten years, I expect, I shall find Sher Ali gone and Maula Bux, the already old *Khansama*, sitting in his place—half-demented with senile decay. And yet, how these lovable characters carry us back into the dim past when our fathers travelled long distances by *dâk-garries* and used these bungalows as stage-houses. What a memory lies behind them! And now, with Railways clattering their way across the country, through hewn forest and tunnelled mountain, over great rivers and expansive deserts, we scarcely see these speaking landmarks of ancient days, except on occasional bursts into the countryside, brought about by absolute necessity. But the Dâk Bungalows of India still call. They call to the weary and the heart-sore, they call to those who are oppressed by the humdrum of life's battle, they call to those who want rest, and their message is a message of peace.

Kurantadih.

(The former Ballia).

I saw it in the Moon's pale light—desolate Kurantadih!
There, like a phantom of the night, it stands in grand solemnity.
The jail-house door is thrown ajar, no sentinel is posted there;
Its crumbling walls loom from afar and face the world with stony stare.
The court-room door is opened wide, no longer now the criminal's way,
Upon the dais no judgment seat, the broken dock an ashen grey.
The Treasury's overgrown with shrubs, no sentry-guard is stationed there:
A jackal, frighted by my step, slinks silent from its covert lair.
I wend my way towards the club, where fifty years and more ago,
The *Sahibs* gathered every day when the Eastern sun was sinking low.
Alas! one room alone withstands the eking out of Time:
The rest, a mass of ruins lie, dishevelled bricks and mouldering lime.

Headquarters of a District once, this pleasant little
station :
Contentment then reigned in this land—not Non-co-
operation.
Enshrouded in a distant haze, in silhouette, I faintly see
The ramparts of a Mogul fort,* the pride of Moslem
history,
O monuments of ancient days! O relics of a glorious
past!
Speaks still thy silent majesty, through winter's wind
and summer's blast.
I leave it with a tender sigh—beautiful Kurantadih!
Would that my Muse could soar enough more fitting
praise to give to thee.

---

* The reference is to the ruined fort at Buxar.

The Indian Witch-Doctor.

FOR the benefit of those who have not themselves seen an Indian Witch-Doctor casting out an evil spirit I record an experience I had one morning. I was strolling along a narrow meandering pathway in the countryside, followed by an old veteran, a villager of 88 hoary years of age but active withal and still in the possession of his senses and his sight. He had a stick in his hand and it was wonderful with what alacrity he hobbled along behind me. The countryside was beautiful, the green fields stretching out on every side like well-kept lawns and adorned here and there with the deep red of the velvety *Ramdana* crop, while the whole scene was swathed in a blue mantle of smoke which emerged from the little village to the east. The old man, in his rustic manner, was recounting to me tales of the Indian Mutiny when he was a boy of 16 years of age. He remembered how he fled with the residents of his village, pursued by the punitive expedition led by Mr. Mayne from Allahabad, how a small detachment of cavalry intercepted their path and how the village of Dobaha was bombarded and burnt because it was a rebel centre. "There is a *pipal* tree a little further ahead," he added, "where the leading rebel of this place was hanged. There it is, *Sahib*, on that patch of *jungle* ahead." "Is that so"? I said. "How interesting! I must go and see it from close quarters." The old man did not reply and seemed to be tiring. After a minute, I said "I'm afraid you're tired,

Ram Anup; you had better not come all that way. I'll go on." Again I got no reply; but without looking back, I knew the old man was shuffling along behind me from the sound of the steadily repeated thud of his stick on the ground. After a long pause, old Ram Anup replied "You are, of course, the *dunya ki malik* (the owner of the world) so you can go there, *Sahib;* but it is very dangerous for one of us". "But why?" I replied, "What's wrong? I suppose you people have placed a *Bhút* (evil spirit) there." "That's *exactly* it, *Sahib,*" he said with animation and emphasis, "Your wisdom is so vast that you knew exactly what was in my mind. We are a foolish people, *Sahib;* but we believe firmly that there is a *Bhút* that hovers under the shadow of that tree. On more than one occasion it has laid hold of those who went too near it." He was so earnest that I restrained my laughter and scorn at the suggestion, and replied "Well, look here, Ram Anup, let me test it. You stand on the borders of the *jungle* patch on which it is situated and watch me while I go and walk all round the tree." "But it won't dare touch you, *Sahib*" he said, "I know it won't. The Englishman is safe. It was the Englishman who hung up the man whose spirit is there. It is the curse of the Englishman on the rebel, so it cannot touch you." As he spoke, I saw a lad of about 14 years of age, with a bundle on his back and a stick across his shoulder, stepping gaily along the road which led to Baraut and passed this tree within a couple of hundred yards. On spying me, his interest was evidently aroused and he deviated from the direction to come towards me. I deliberately altered the course I was pursuing by a slight incline so that the tree lay between me and the boy. Then I stopped and waited. Though the old man's story had rung of sincerity, I just wished to see if the boy would avoid the tree in approaching me; but he did not. He came straight forward in my direction. Nearer and nearer to the tree he approached. Now he was almost under it. The old man's frail eyesight could not perceive his approach, and I was waiting for the moment when the boy was right under the branches to draw Ram Anup's attention to it and say to him "See, there's an Indian and only a lad. He has neither attempted to avoid the tree nor has anything affected him". The boy came on with jocund step and now he was in the deepest shade of the tree. "Look!" I said, "Ram Anup, look, there's that boy—". Suddenly, the boy crumpled up as if struck by lightning. His bundle and his stick went rolling aside. His body was contorted into the most terrible shape. One knee was drawn up near his chin which was thrown back and his arms were twisted behind him. He seemed to be writhing in agony. The paroxysm was terrible. It was all the matter of a second and I seemed to lose all power of speech for that momentary period. The suddenness, the swiftness with which the boy was struck down, left me powerless, just for the moment, to realise the situation or to decide what should be done. "The boy has fainted under the tree, Ram Anup," I said excitedly, "Send for water quick." "What boy? where?" said Ram Anup in alarm and surprise. "Under the tree. Quick!" I said, as I advanced towards the poor youngster. I did not look back at Ram Anup, but I could hear his weak voice behind me calling to someone in the fields some distance away. When I reached the boy, I was certain it was an epileptic attack. His eyelids were quivering at a terrible rate, showing beneath them a pair of blood-shot eyes. His whole body was twisting backwards: I was powerless to help him. In a very short time, a general alarm was raised and people gathered from the surrounding fields, but none dared come nearer than the border of the *jungle* patch where Ram Anup and I had stood. " Bring water," I called out and someone pretended to run off for it. Suddenly a man, an Ahir, arrived with deep-sunk cheeks and hollowed eyes. He was the witch-doctor. I didn't know his position, and I demanded rather impatiently of him " Where's the water ? I want water to put on this boy's head. What will I do with *you* ? " He took no notice whatever of me, but sat down on his haunches, his eyes fixed on the boy, his elbows resting on his knees, his fingers entwined and held against his nose, his lips mumbling something rapidly and earnestly. Every now and again, he would utter a sharp guttural sound while his whole body would give a convulsive twitch. It was like a super-hiccough ; but it was more weird than farcical. The mumbling sounds became more distinct. I could hear the words " Ram " and *Bhawani* and *Jah* in amongst a volume of other jumbled sounds and half-articulate words. His twitchings became more severe, the muscles of his whole body were standing out like ropes, his fingers alternately gripped and straightened out like pieces of card-board. His excitement increased to a frenzied extent and as it increased, the boy's convulsive movements decreased. And now, the witch-doctor seemed to be swept into a typhoon of passion, his body was palpitating, his head was wagging furiously from side to side, his lips were trembling then firmly compressed, his voice rose higher and higher in angry tones, breaking out every now and then with a shriek of fuming rage as he said *Jah*. And all the time his eyes were fixed upon the boy. Now, suddenly, his voice would fall and he would seem to groan in agony, then with osculating sound from his lips he would seem to be coaxing a wild horse. Another shout of consuming passion, then he gripped his nose, muttering as he did so and pleading "I won't do it again; I won't do it again." Another loud *Jah*, then further pleading followed by vile abuse in which every female relative of the evil spirit was dishonoured. The boy was now lying with widely-opened eyes, staring vacantly upwards as calmly as if he had arisen from the stupor of a deep sleep. Gradually, the passion of the witch-doctor abated as his 'victory' over the evil one increased. Gradually, his composure returned as the *Bhút* pleaded for mercy and promised not "to do it again." Then, he suddenly ceased operating and the strange look from his eye had gone as he commanded the boy "Get up and get away from under this tree." The boy rose slowly, but would have fallen if I had not helped him to the village people where they stood. To my surprise no one recognised him. He was not of the village; but was a passer-by along the way. He described himself as an orphan and resident of a village in the Benares State. No wonder, then, that he did not know of the lurking evil spirit which held sway under that fateful *pipal* tree. He was surprised when I asked him if he was subject to these fits. He asserted he had never had one before, which is extraordinary, if the fit was epileptic. Perhaps, old Ram Anup is right and the 'owner of the world' is wrong.

The

Thanadar

OR

Sub-Inspector of Police.

I see him on his charger fair,
With Sam Browne belt and martial air,
A lion from his *Thana* lair,
It is the *Thanadar*.

I see him as he rides along,
Ensample of the brave and strong,
With quickened eye for every wrong,
The much-feared *Thanadar*.

Let those abuse who blindly will,
With biting tongue and wicked quill,
His sins and faults; we need him still,
The good old *Thanadar*.

His *Thana* stands a stronghold grand,
Feared by the criminal of the land;
True emblem of the Law's strong hand,
Home of the *Thanadar*,

'Tis there, by these cold whited walls,
The rustic, seeking justice, calls;
And stricken grief before him falls,
Before the *Thanadar*.

To them, he represents the might,
Of British Justice and of Right.
God grant him strength to use aright,
The powers of *Thanadar*.

The Romance of an Indian Wedding.

IT has been estimated that no less than a million marriages were celebrated in India during the month of March, 1930. This orgy of unions between children of tender ages was, of course, the result of the new legislation to put a stop to child-marriages after 1st April, 1930. We witnessed many processions and realised vaguely that they represented "marriages," but we were largely ignorant of many interesting phases in an Indian wedding. I touch on a few here.

While the Christian marriage is almost entirely a religious affair, the Indian marriage still has a touch of the romantic in it and takes us back to the time when the bridegroom set forth with martial accompaniment to seize the lady of his choice by armed force. He was accompanied by armed men and horses and elephants in all the panoply of war. He himself was in full war-paint being daubed from head to foot with saffron. Along with him went tray-bearers carrying presents for his bride, should he succeed in capturing her. Thus it is that to this day the bridegroom carries with him all the paraphernalia he does in what is known as the *barat*. When he reaches the limits of the village in which the bride resides, his camp stops in a grove and throughout the night, in mimic warfare, martial music is played and trumpeters sound the clarion-call for an imaginary battle. Lest an unexpected attack on the camp is made, the party sits up till the early hours of the morning, entertained by music and dancing. The father of the bride collects his people and music is played at his door as if to answer the challenge of the raider who has come to seize his daughter. Then, next day, the bridegroom, mounted on a horse, boldy rides up to the door of the bride's house accompanied by his supporters. He is bedecked in all the finery of a prince and wears, upon his head, a crown something like the King of Siam. On his arrival, the father of the bride capitulates and does honour to the conquering hero by worshipping him and touching his feet in front of the sacred fire. This is called the *Ghar dwari Puja* (the worship at the door of the house). From that day onwards, neither the bride's father nor her mother can eat or drink in the village of the bridegroom. This is in keeping with the idea that the parents of the bride are disgraced by the seizure of their daughter by a man who would make her his wife. Thus the position of the parents-in-law of the bride is practically a reversal of the accepted position in European society where the proposing bridegroom-to-be always finds a place, in comic pictures, on the tip of the boot of the irate father of the fair maiden and the mother-in-law is the bane of his life!

The following night, the bridegroom enters the house of his bride alone, leaving his own followers outside. The family of his bride makes him welcome and the bride is brought out, coyly hiding her face. They both sit round a sacred fire at which the priests preside. After much chanting of prayers, the corner of the bride's *sari* (robe) is tied to the corner of the bridegroom's shirt. This is the marriage knot and thus united, the bridal couple move slowly round the sacred fire seven times while the bride's relatives shower puffed rice on her. This corresponds with the throwing of confetti on the bridal couple. The ceremony is called the *Bhaunri* and is one of the most important. In the matter of inheritance of property, whole States are lost or won on the proof or otherwise of the performance of this essential ceremony. Following this, is the *Senduria* ceremony which is almost equally as important as the *Bhaunri*. Here the bridegroom dips his finger in a red powder (called *Senduria*) and after each prayer by the *Pandit* (or priest), he makes a mark on the middle of the bride's forehead. This he repeats seven times. It is because of the ceremony that we see that every married woman amongst Hindus always wears a red mark from her forehead backwards along the part of her hair. A spinster or a widow cannot wear this distinctive mark and hence it is always possible in a crowd to pick out the married women whose husbands are living.

The third night's ceremony is called the *Baharia* (the outsiders) and on this night, the bridegroom's party freely fraternises with the party of the bride. A feast is given to the whole gathering by the father of the bride. This is his final humiliation and his final acknowledgment of his defeat. This done, the victorious bridegroom, riding his horse, proceeds homewards, his bride following in a completely covered palanquin and behind her all his mace-bearers and relatives. This is called the *Bida* (or the send-off).

The Indian Fortune-Teller.

[THE Indian fortune-teller of the type represented below belongs to a class of savants and quacks that is rapidly passing out. Nearly every Englishman in India, especially the British soldier, will recollect meeting him at one time or another. His phraseology is always distinctive and his predictions invariably stereotyped.]

He comes with mystic air
In flowing turmeric robes
With strings and strings of beads
And ear-rings on his lobes.

" I tell it Master's fortune,"
He says in accents mild,
" You'll have it too much money
And plenty wife and child."

He places on my palm,
A dirty string of dice
And tells me all my past
As he heard it from the *syce*.*

He speaks of great promotion
Of lucky stars and bad
He tells me where I'll go
And just when I'll be 'had.'

He gives the same old yarn
And tells me very soon,
I'll be pompous General
On the " thirty-first " of June!

---

* *Syce*=groom.

In The Indian Jungle.

SHIKAR stories are so common and usually so exaggerated that it makes me hesitate to describe my own experience. In view of this, however, I shall attempt to be as precise as possible so that no hyperbole may creep into the account.

It was a lovely sunlit May day in the hills that I set out to make a local inspection seven miles from Naini Tal. On the way I met one of my subordinate officials, a *Patwari*, to whom I mentioned, in the course of conversation, that it was time he gave me information about the whereabouts of a tiger which I could shoot. "Impossible in these parts at the present time of the year," he said dejectedly "but in the winter," he added, "there will be plenty of opportunities." The words had hardly escaped his lips when, by one of the strangest coincidences I know, a villager hailed out "*Patwari Ji*! Does the Sahib know that a tiger killed a cow two miles away last night?" The *Patwari's* lips curled with disgusted incredulity as he turned to me and said "It is just like these people, *Sahib*. He has discovered you want to shoot a tiger and he thinks it will please you immensely if he gives you a yarn like that. It is an obvious untruth." The villager overheard him as he came nearer, and cried "It is not untrue, I assure you, *Patwari Ji*. I have seen the tiger at the carcase only this morning. I saw him with my own eyes." The *Patwari* now looked angry and said "You add absurdity to falsehood. The idea of a tiger eating a 'kill' by day." I felt, however, that the villager was telling the truth and I said

'If it is only two miles, let us go and see, anyhow. "Very well, *Sahib*" replied the *Patwari*, "but we must take this man with us and make him swallow his own words if he takes us on a wild-goose-chase, which I am sure he is doing." So off we went. "Now we are near the spot," whispered the villager and he was obviously nervous. We mounted the crest of the hill and as we did so, there we saw the carcase of a cow lying down in the valley twenty yards below us. We walked right on as the *Patwari* said "You see, *Sahib*, there's no tiger, this is probably an animal which has died of—God! there it is!" and he dropped to the ground as if he had been shot. There, within 15 yards of us, was a tiger which rose slowly from behind the carcase and slouched away up the thickly wooded ravine. I seized the *Patwari's* gun and brought it to my shoulder when the villager grasped my arm exclaiming in hushed and excited voice:

"For God's sake don't shoot, *Sahib*. It will kill us all. You can shoot it from a *machan* this evening." I restrained myself and I only now know how providential it was that I did.

I then sent for my brother from Naini Tal and meanwhile had two *machans* prepared. Evening came, and we climbed into our own respective *machans* on different trees. These were wonderfully well-made, so completely enwrapped in leaves that no one could tell that they could form the temporary lair of a human being. And then our men departed. We were alone in the forest. It was evening and the sun was just dropping down over the crest of the hill. The twitter of the birds of the forest gradually died away. The silence increased and was broken only by the occasional creeking of crickets. In the intervals the hush was wonderful. I could hear the distant mountain stream like a long-continued sigh. A leaf fluttered down from the tree on which I sat and the sound as it touched the ground was like a distant crash. I passed my hand across my face and even that gentle movement sounded like the rustling of paper. The silence was majestic, as we waited with eyes intently fixed on the silent carcase of the cow lying in weird and deathful stillness.

Our guns were focussed on the corpse as the time passed slowly on. Dare we move in the slightest and a tell-tale rustle would instantly be created. I could hear my very breath. And then suddenly, after nearly two hours' waiting, just as dusk was setting in, there was a slight shuffling noise and the tiger appeared. For a moment, he stood still and watched the "kill." Then, with a light spring, he was on it. A tremendous report rang out into the silent evening air. My brother had fired, and almost simultaneously, I too pulled my trigger. He was obviously hit. I had expected a terrible roar from the animal as he leapt up into the air. But there was only a vicious choking growl and then, spotting my brother, he charged his tree. So madly reckless was his onslaught that he stumbled and fell in the intervening ravine. My brother fired again but missed on this occasion. Up the tiger rose and continued his charge, leaping up repeatedly towards my brother's *machan*, and shredding the bark from the tree. I have heard the words "rage," and "passion" applied to human beings; but this was a rage and a passion that I could never have conceived. The animal was trembling all over his agile frame, tearing at the base of the tree, audibly fuming. Unfortunately the tree which stood between my brother's *machan* and mine prevented me from seeing him at this moment to enable me to shoot, but I could hear all the varied sounds of his mad anger and attempts to scale the tree. My brother, too, could not see him to fire, as he was directly under his *machan*, hidden also by thick shrub. For half-an-hour or more he vented his agonised wrath on the base of the tree, the heavy breathing gradually died away and we decided he was either dead or had decamped. Darkness had now set in. We fired two shots into the ground below us as a precautionary measure preparatory to coming down, and as there was no response, we descended from our respective perches. With the utmost caution we returned to the village determined to stay there the night and trace the tiger next morning. We slept under a little thatched roof and early next morning proceeded to the "kill." We could distinctly see the blood marks the tiger had left behind and judging from the quantity of blood we saw splattered about everywhere we decided he must have laid down and died not very far off from that spot. Up the valley we went, stumbling over rocks and boulders, deeper and deeper into the forest, following every spot of blood. And then the valley became so narrow that we could only walk in single file. I was at the head of this solemn procession, behind me was a local landlord named Bachi Singh, then my brother, followed by half-a-dozen villagers.

We must have proceeded thus for half-a-mile when suddenly from the thicket straight in front of us and only five yards away there was a whining gurgling noise followed by a muffled "woof." A tawny-coloured streak shot out of the thicket. There was no time to speak, there was hardly time to act; but I instinctively brought my gun up to my shoulder and fired. It was my right barrel which bore lethal. I do not mind admitting that at that moment I was the most excited—perhaps the most frightened—man in Asia. My gun.

was wobbling before me and, needless to add, I missed. In the next moment, the tiger stood rampant before me and I fired my left barrel into its mouth. It lashed out at me viciously, just grazing the hand with which I supported my gun. It was at that moment I realised as never before what it is to be face to face with death. I cannot describe the feeling of utter helplessness, the feeling of numbness that overpowered my brain, the feeling of complete resignation. My mind simply stopped working. There was, for a brief moment, a complete cessation of thought. And then realisation suddenly returned, and I shouted to the Forest Guard for more cartridges. He had fled incontinently and then up stood the tiger again and lashed out at Bachi Singh, smashing his gun into three pieces. Almost simultaneously it had grasped Bachi Singh round the shoulders and rolled over with him on to the ground. A sickening sound of the crackling of bones emerged from the bloody maelstrom near my feet while blood splashed out freely and covered my clothes. I shouted to my brother "We're finished ; but fire if you can." The words were hardly out of my mouth when I discovered that Bachi Singh and the tiger had fallen on to my brother. There he lay rolling and writhing, Bachi Singh on him and the tiger over both. My catridges finished, no hope of getting any more immediately, I waited for my turn. My feeling was that it would not take long to see the tiger finish both of them off and then finish me. Instinctively I stood with the gun to my shoulder. After a few seconds—which seemed like years—the tiger turned on me, looked into the barrels of my gun, winced and bounded away into the thicket nearby. Quickly we got Bachi Singh away to the hospital. Both his arms from the elbows down had been chewed up.

My brother escaped with a few scratches. Our followers had all decamped except for my Orderly whom I sent off to collect men and guns to beat out the animal. To leave him would have been unconscionable for the very sound of the human voice to a wounded tiger—particularly one that had tasted of the sweetness of human blood—would have meant death to the unwary victim.

A little later the men arrived and we commenced our march up the narrow valley stretched out in line, pushing our way through thorny thickets and closely-grown shurbs. We had only gone a few paces when once again the tiger shot out and vigorously slapped a beater across the head, tearing away half his scalp. And as he fell, the tiger jumped on to his back and tore his coat to shreds springing round again and biting viciously at his legs. None of us dare shoot lest we perchance hit the beater. But in the next second, the tiger leapt off and as he did so two reports rang out into the silent forest air. The tiger fell to the ground writhing in his death-struggles, rolling to the bottom of the valley and lying still. My shot had gone through his heart and my brother's through his head. Cautiously we approached it and then we had the only joke of the day. The tiger was a tigress—and a magnificent specimen at that. We discovered now that my brother's shot of the previous evening had broken its jawbone and this alone saved our lives. But danger has its thrills, consequently its attractions and the incident has only made me long for a repetition of similar excitement. It is not courage, it is just madness—but it is an ecstatic madness withal.

"Watchman ! What of the Night ?"

The sun of a happy India set
In the golden west of the summer sky ;
We had hardly the time to wish it adieu
Or to whisper a last good-bye.

And the moon shot up in the azure vault-
What is that we see in the paling light ?
The doors of the prisons are thrown ajar ;
In front—a host in spotless white.

I turn to the man who stands at the gate
And ask him, " Watchman, what of the night ? "
" God only knows, " he makes reply,
" Pray for the dawn ! Pray for light ! "

PIONEER PRESS, ALLAHABAD, No. 290—25-7-'30—300.